GREGG R. ALL

GOD
GIFT
AND
GUIDE

KNOWING
THE HOLY SPIRIT

PUBLISHING
BRENTWOOD, TENNESSEE

DEDICATION

I dedicate this book to Brad and Jill House, dear friends. Jill, you showed courage through struggle as you trusted the sovereignty of God. Your faithful support for Brad and trusting concern for your children are exemplary. Thank you for your listening ear and love for Nora and me.

Brad, you never sway from speaking truth and sharing wisdom. The Holy Spirit gave you direction for me at the right time. Writing a book together, enjoying Simon and Garfunkel music, and cheering for our respective teams—Detroit for you, Chicago for me—are great joys.

I love and appreciate you both!

CONTENTS

PRAYER TO THE HOLY SPIRIT (FROM AUGUSTINE, 354–430)

Breathe in me, O Holy Spirit, that
my thoughts may all be holy;

Act in me, O Holy Spirit, that my
works, too, may be holy;

Draw my heart, O Holy Spirit,
that I love but what is holy;

Strengthen me, O Holy Spirit,
to defend all that is holy;

Guard me, then, O Holy Spirit,
that I always may be holy.

CHAPTER 1

The Wonderful Discovery

As I made my way to the meeting, I wondered what the evening had in store for me. Little did I know that the Holy Spirit would transform my life forever.

I had become a Christian about a year and a half earlier. Though raised in a church, I had never believed the gospel: that Jesus Christ had died on the cross to pay the penalty for my sins and had risen from the dead to accomplish my salvation. While that experience in embracing Christ was quite dramatic, the feelings that arose from my conversion wore off several months later. This disappointment was true not only for me but for the sixty or so other high school friends who had made professions of faith that same weekend in October. We concluded that we had tried Christianity, and it had failed us.

We went our separate ways to different universities the following fall. One of my friends, Jim, who had become a Christian the same weekend I had, wrote me a series of letters—eleven unanswered letters. He urged me to check out a group called Campus

Crusade for Christ (now Cru) because it had helped him to live for Jesus Christ.

My first semester of freshman year, I had no interest in heeding the encouragement of my friend. At the start of my second semester, however, mired in a typical freshman crisis, I determined I needed to find Cru and attend one of its meetings. When I spied a flyer with information about a Thursday evening Cru get together in one of the residence halls, my interest was piqued.

As I made my way to the meeting, my introverted nature began to kick in. I had strong doubts that Cru would be for me. Still, I continued on, eventually entering the doors of the dorm. What I saw only confirmed my suspicions: a bunch of weird-looking students were milling around, talking and smiling. They had huge crosses hanging from their necks and strange pins attached to their shirts and blouses that read: "one way," "Jesus is a bridge over troubled waters," "in case of rapture," "my leader is a Jewish carpenter." Definitely strange!

About ready to pivot and exit the door from which I had just entered, I glanced at a hulk of a man, Chris, standing near me. He had a flaming red afro and a long red beard. Spying me, and perhaps sensing my doubts, he beckoned with his index finger for me to come his way. Mesmerized, I drew near to him and, mysteriously, entered into the meeting room where Cru was about to start its worship time.

After a few songs, prayers, and announcements, the leader of Cru, Steve, directed us to choose one of several breakout sessions to attend. One session title intrigued me because I wanted to find out the answer to its question: "Have you ever made the wonderful discovery of the Spirit-filled life?" What "Spirit-filled" meant, I had no idea. But it sounded interesting, so I moved to the room in which the session was being held.

An hour later, I had come to the realization that God never intended for me to try to live the Christian life in my own power and by my own efforts. Following Jesus was impossible by trying hard by myself. Quite the contrary: God had provided all the resources for me to live for Jesus, and I needed to rely on what He had provided. One essential resource was the Holy Spirit. Not only had He been key in my conversion. He had come to dwell within me, and through relying on Him, I would be able to live a life that is fully pleasing to God. So, at the end of that session, I asked the Holy Spirit to fill me.

I made the wonderful discovery of the Spirit-filled life!

That critical moment was the turning point in my Christian life. It propelled me, together with the woman who would later become my wife, to work on Cru staff for eighteen years. To this day, it compels me to teach, speak, and write on the Holy Spirit. That wonderful discovery of the Spirit-filled life is the reason why this book is so personal for me and why it is so important for me to share with you about the Holy Spirit.

If you have not already done so, maybe you, too, will make the wonderful discovery of the Spirit-filled life! To aid in this discovery or deepen the understanding you already have, read the following chapters with a pen in hand and journal nearby. At times you will be guided to reflect or respond. Don't skip those instances. May God use them to magnify the Spirit-filled life!

CHAPTER 2

The Good Gift

Now that I've told you a bit of my story, let's consider your own story. As you look back over the course of your Christian life, how can you account for the growth that you see? Whether you're a fairly new Christian or a longtime follower of Christ, how can you explain the progress you've experienced over the course of days, weeks, months, years, or maybe even decades? Grab a notebook or journal and list what has attributed to your growth as a Christian.

If I can guess your list, it probably contains items such as:

- *the Bible:* reading, memorizing, studying, praying, and applying the Word of God
- *prayer:* reciting the Lord's Prayer, praising and thanking God, voicing requests for yourself and for others, and interceding for concerns at your church

- *church:* worship, singing, confessing sin, giving, listening to sermons, and celebrating baptism and the Lord's Supper
- *small group participation:* studying the Bible together with others, fellowshipping with other church members in a community group, engaging in outreach as part of a missional community
- *spiritual disciplines:* fasting, silence, journaling, accountability, and retreats
- *service:* using your spiritual gifts (such as teaching, leading, administrating, and exhorting) at church, evangelizing, discipling new believers, counseling those in crisis, and supporting missions
- *life events:* suffering, forgiving others, celebrating milestones (such as graduations, marriages, and births), and grieving tragedies (such as dire medical prognoses, onset of Alzheimer's, and deaths)

Because of what I've shared in my story, I'm going to guess that your list includes another important item that helps account for your growth as a Christian over the course of time:

- *the Holy Spirit:* being filled with the Spirit, walking in the Spirit, keeping in step with the Spirit, setting your mind on the things of the Spirit, and being guided by the Spirit of God

To press this point a bit more: What would we be missing if there were no Holy Spirit? If He had never existed? If He had somehow disappeared? Make this a second list in your notebook or journal.

I hope you have lots of items on your list. Here are some of mine:

- the existence of the world and everything it contains, including you and me
- awareness of our sin and need for Jesus to save us
- the new birth (or regeneration) and conversion, that is, becoming a Christian
- acknowledging that Jesus is Lord
- being united with Christ, justified (declared not guilty but righteous instead), and adopted by God
- being sealed as a guarantee of our salvation
- the assurance of our salvation
- sanctification, or progressive maturity in the Christian life
- the ability to understand and apply the Bible to our life
- prayer for God to help us in our deepest times of need
- unity in our church
- leaders for our church
- evangelism and mission through our church
- spiritual gifts benefiting our church
- (in the future) our resurrection bodies
- (in the future) the new heaven and new earth

What would we be missing if there were no Holy Spirit? In a word: everything! (And as we go through this book, I'll show you how the Holy Spirit relates to all these blessings.)

In my experience, this answer is not the one many Christians would give to that question. I find much confusion about the Holy Spirit, along with a lot of fear of the Holy Spirit.

But why? Why is there confusion, hesitancy, ignorance, anxiety, worry, and fear when it comes to the Spirit of God?

To start with, some Christians wonder who the Holy Spirit is. Is the Spirit fully God, equal to God the Father and God the Son? Or is He less than the Father and the Son, a kind of junior god hoping to one day be called from the developmental squad to be on the pro team along with the Father and the Son?

Is the Spirit a person—not a human person, but a divine person? Or is the Spirit a force, a power, an influence? After all, it's fairly easy to understand the personhood of the other two simply by considering their names: Father (clearly a person) and Son (clearly a person). But what about the Spirit? Not clearly a person, perhaps closer to a strength (we often say, "Yeah, that's the spirit") or closer to vigor (we may say, "She's in good spirits!"). And (without wishing to offend anyone) the traditional name "Holy Ghost" conjures up visits from ghouls and spooks on Halloween. They are certainly not divine! So is the Holy Spirit just the power of God?

If we believe that the Holy Spirit is a divine person, equal to God the Father and God the Son, then should we worship the Holy Spirit? In the same way and to the same extent that we worship the Father and the Son? Should we trust and obey the Holy Spirit? In the same way and to the same extent that we trust and obey the Father and the Son? Should we pray to the Holy Spirit? In the same way and to the same extent that we pray to the Father and the Son?

Should we seek to glorify the Holy Spirit? In the same way and to the same extent that we seek to glorify the Father and the Son?

Let's bring this discussion (and our list of questions could be much, much longer) to an end. There is confusion and hesitancy about the Holy Spirit because some wonder who He is.

There is also uncertainty and caution about the Holy Spirit because some Christians wonder what the Holy Spirit does. Recall our list above: conviction of sin, the new birth, sealing, assurance of salvation, resurrection, and so forth. Could we say that, from the beginning of our Christian life, through its ongoing progress, and all the way to the end, the Holy Spirit is actively engaged in all that we are, do, and will become? If that is true, then we're once again faced with our question: Why do some Christians hear so little and know so little about Him? And why is there confusion about the Holy Spirit?

Sadly, more than just confusion and ignorance reigns in regard to the Holy Spirit's work among God's people. Fear sometimes grips Christians' hearts as well. It may be fear of themselves—that they will be manipulated or, worse, may offend God. Or it may be fear of giving up control of their life—because they doubt that God is good. When they read the book of Acts or hear stories of missionaries throughout church history, they feel dread, worry, and distress: If I (or my children, or my best friends) truly surrender my (their) life to the guidance of the Holy Spirit, who knows what may happen! I (they) may end up like the apostle Paul or the early martyrs or the missionaries working in closed countries where being a Christ-follower brings the sentence of death. "No, thank you," is the uneasy reply. It is better to live a compromised Christian life and be comfortable and safe rather than submit completely to the Spirit's call.

I get it. Early on in our marriage, my wife and I committed ourselves to go anywhere, say anything, do anything, and give up everything—cost what it may cost—to follow the Spirit's leading. Within two years, we left our country, said goodbye to our families and many friends, and walked away from a flourishing ministry at the University of Notre Dame. We settled into a new country (Italy), new language (we studied Italian in Florence), new culture, new friends, and became involved in a new ministry in Rome and, later, the Italian-speaking part of Switzerland. Much to our embarrassment, we slipped often on cultural banana peels. We confused *tonno* (tuna) and *tuono* (thunder) such that during a violent storm, we exclaimed, "What tuna!" when we heard the clash of thunder. We continuously balked—and backed away—when Italians put their face so close to our face during conversations with us—different social space from our American custom. At times, our lives and ministries were exhilarating, eclipsing anything we had experienced before. At other times, we were confused, exasperated, frustrated, lonely, and misunderstood. Saying yes to the Spirit's guidance was costly—but very worth it.

It is this fear of what it may cost that paralyzes many Christians and prevents them from yielding fully to the Holy Spirit. So, we ignore the Spirit's tugging at our heart or close off ourselves from seeking His direction.

There is confusion, hesitancy, ignorance, anxiety, worry, and fear when it comes to the Spirit of God. Rather than surrender consistently and continuously to Him, we quench the Holy Spirit, in disobedience to Paul's warning (1 Thess. 5:19 ESV).

If we think about Jesus's teaching about the Holy Spirit, such a posture doesn't make any sense. In His Sermon on the Mount, Jesus addresses the goodness of His Father—who is our Father too.

Jesus starts with an analogy with earthly—even evil—parents: they would never give their children a stone rather than bread or a serpent rather than a fish. He then extends the point to our heavenly Father: "If you then, who are evil, know how to give good gifts to your children, how much more will your Father who is in heaven *give good things* to those who ask him" (Matt. 7:11).

Interestingly, Luke's Gospel switches up the last promise about giving "good things": "If you then, who are evil, know how to give good gifts to your children, how much more will the heavenly Father *give the Holy Spirit* to those who ask him?" (Luke 11:13).

Give good gifts.

Give the Holy Spirit.

Here's my claim: *The greatest gift that God the Father gives to those who follow His Son is the Holy Spirit.* That is, at the very top of the list of the "good gifts" that the Father gives to us Christians is the Holy Spirit.

> The greatest gift that God the Father gives to those who follow His Son is the Holy Spirit.

I can already hear the objection: But the Bible says that the greatest gift of all is Jesus—His death and resurrection for our salvation! I couldn't agree more! But while agreeing with the objection, I continue to hold this claim as true. It addresses those who have already received the greatest gift of all—salvation through Jesus—and makes a further claim: for those who follow God's Son, Jesus, the greatest gift that the Father gives to them is the Holy Spirit. Those who receive the gift of salvation receive another gift, the greatest of the "good gifts" for Christians: the Spirit of God.

If my claim is true and we Christians have the gift of the Holy Spirit, why is there so much confusion and fear about Him? For Christians to be perplexed over who this gift is—fully God or junior god, a divine person or a powerful force, the "all" of our Christian life or just some aspect—that just doesn't make any sense. For Christians to be afraid of fully embracing this gift—that just doesn't make any sense. It grieves God the Father, who is the giver of this gift. It grieves God the Son, who promised, "It is for your benefit that I go away, because if I don't go away the Counselor [the Holy Spirit] will not come to you. If I go, I will send him to you" (John 16:7). It "grieves the Holy Spirit of God, by whom you were sealed for the day of redemption" (Eph. 4:30 ESV).

We don't want to grieve God, who is Father, Son, and Holy Spirit. On the contrary, let us embrace the greatest gift that God the Father gives to those who follow His Son: the Holy Spirit.

Time for a bit of self-reflection. Each chapter will end in an opportunity for you to reflect, so keep that journal and pen near.

1. How important a role do you assign to the Holy Spirit as you seek to account for your growth as a Christian over the course of time? Does your realization of this absent/limited/ significant role surprise you? Why or why not?

2. Have you ever experienced ignorance about and/or confusion over the Holy Spirit? Do you consider Him to be fully God, a divine person rather than a mighty influence? Do you worship the Holy Spirit? Trust and obey Him? Seek to glorify Him? Why or why not?

3. Do you fear yielding fully to the Holy Spirit? What causes such hesitancy in seeking His guidance for your life? Can you point to specific times in which you've withdrawn from following His direction? What can you do to rectify this wrong posture so as not to grieve the Holy Spirit?

4. Do you agree or disagree with my claim: the greatest gift that God the Father gives to those who follow His Son is the Holy Spirit? How does your answer affect your Christian life?

I believe in
the Holy Spirit,
the Lord and
Giver of Life,
who proceeds from
the Father and the Son,
who with the Father
and the Son together
is worshipped and glorified.

—Nicene-Constantinopolitan
Creed (381)

PART 1

Worshipping God the Holy Spirit

This book is divided into three sections: Worshipping God the Holy Spirit, Walking with God the Holy Spirit, and Working with God the Holy Spirit. The first—and by far the longest—section centers on the identity and works of the Holy Spirit. As a divine person (chap. 3) of the Trinity (chap. 4) who engages in divine works (chaps. 5–12), He is worthy of our worship.

The second section turns to how we as Christians are to walk with the Holy Spirit, who fills us with the presence of the triune God (chap. 13), gives us life (chap. 14), and guides us to do God's will (chap. 15).

The third—and shortest—section focuses on how we work with the Holy Spirit by highlighting His earlier works (chap. 16), and explaining His gifts (chap. 17), some of which are debated (chap. 18). At the end of each chapter are questions for self-reflection, personal transformation, and/or application for your church. The conclusion draws together these three sections.

The Spirit's Divine Person

The following two chapters focus on two key truths about the Holy Spirit's divine personhood. Chapter 3 presents the identity of the Holy Spirit. He is fully God, the divine Third Person of the Trinity. He is not defective in deity, nor lesser than the Father and the Son. And He is a person rather than a power, force, or influence.

Chapter 4 discusses how the Holy Spirit, while being equal to the Father and the Son, is distinguished from these other two divine persons. Following a basic primer on the Trinity, the eternal procession and temporal mission of the Holy Spirit is highlighted.

CHAPTER 3

The Holy Spirit Is Fully God

The church, from its very beginning, has been Trinitarian, affirming that God eternally exists as Father, Son, and Holy Spirit. We find this Trinitarian orientation on the pages of the New Testament, such as Paul's apostolic blessing: "The grace of the Lord Jesus Christ, and the love of God, and the fellowship of the Holy Spirit be with you all" (2 Cor. 13:13). Salvation begins with the Trinity and brings Christians home to the Trinity, as Paul rehearses: "When the time came to completion, *God sent his Son*, born of a woman, born under the law, to redeem those under the law, so that we might receive adoption as sons. And because you are sons, *God sent the Spirit of his Son* into our hearts, crying, '*Abba, Father!*'" (Gal. 4:4–6).[1] Here, the three-in-one saves us: God (the Father), the Father-sent Son, and the Holy Spirit (the Spirit of the Father's Son). Baptism of new believers is administered "in the name of the

---

1. For further discussion, see Fred Sanders, *The Deep Things of God: How the Trinity Changes Everything*, 2nd ed. (Wheaton, IL: Crossway, 2017).

Father and of the Son and of the Holy Spirit" (Matt. 28:19). God is triune.

The church, from its very beginning, has also been conscious of the person and work of the Holy Spirit. As an example, one of the earliest Christian writings outside of the New Testament offered this praise of church members: "a profound and abundant peace was given to you all, and you had an insatiable desire for doing good, while a full outpouring of the Holy Spirit was upon you all."[2]

Fittingly, then, the earliest church creeds, or confession of the Christian faith, had a Trinitarian structure to them: they affirm belief in God the Father, God the Son, and God the Holy Spirit. Perhaps you are familiar with the Apostles' Creed, which confesses belief "in God the Father Almighty . . . and in Jesus Christ, his only Son, our Lord . . . and in the Holy Spirit." Another early creed, the Nicene-Constantinopolitan Creed, expands on the church's affirmation of the Holy Spirit:

> I believe in the Holy Spirit, the Lord and Giver
> of Life, who proceeds from the Father and the
> Son, who with the Father and the Son together
> is worshipped and glorified, who spoke by the
> prophets.[3]

We note three important truths about the Holy Spirit that the church, from its beginning, has believed.

---

2. Clement of Rome, *First Letter to the Corinthians*, ch. 2. *ANF* 1:5.

3. Nicene-Constantinopolitan Creed (381), with the addition "and the Son" from the Third Synod of Toledo (Spain) in 589. The Western church—the Roman Catholic Church and Protestant churches—affirms the addition of "and the Son," while Eastern Orthodox churches do not.

First, the Holy Spirit is the third person of the Trinity, equal in terms of nature, power, and glory with the Father (the first person) and the Son (the second person). Thus,

whatever we may affirm of the Father:

> he is all-powerful, everywhere present, all-knowing, eternal, independent, loving, just, unchanging, truthful, faithful, wise, holy, good, and more;

we may equally affirm of the Son:

> he is all-powerful, everywhere present, all-knowing, eternal, independent, loving, just, unchanging, truthful, faithful, wise, holy, good, and more;

and we may equally affirm of the Holy Spirit:

> he is all-powerful, everywhere present, all-knowing, eternal, independent, loving, just, unchanging, truthful, faithful, wise, holy, good, and more.[4]

Wait a minute! Isn't the Father just a *little more powerful* than the Son and the Spirit? Isn't the Son just a *little more loving* than the Father and the Spirit? Isn't the Spirit just a *little more holy* than the Father and the Son? No. NO. *No. NO.* **No. NO!**

---

4. Adapted from Gregg R. Allison and Andreas J. Köstenberger, *The Holy Spirit: Theology for the People of God* (Nashville: B&H Academic, 2020), 238.

There is NO difference whatsoever between the three persons of the Trinity in terms of their nature, their attributes, or their divine characteristics. The Father, the Son, and the Holy Spirit cannot be distinguished in any way according to their power, truthfulness, knowledge, justice, independence, and more. They are the three co-eminent persons of the Trinity.

This truth leads to the next one.

Second, the Holy Spirit is to be worshipped and glorified together with the Father and the Son.

The co-eminence of the third person with the first person and the second person means that the praise, honor, adoration, obedience, trust, and thanksgiving that we direct to the Spirit does not differ in essence—in any way, shape, and form—from those same activities directed toward the Father and the Son. That is,

- We praise God the Father to the same extent and with the same fervor that we praise God the Son and God the Holy Spirit.
- We honor the Son to the same extent and with the same fervor that we honor the Father and the Holy Spirit.
- We adore the Holy Spirit to the same extent and with the same fervor that we adore the Father and the Son.

To emphasize still:

- We obey God the Father to the same extent and with the same fervor that we obey God the Son and God the Holy Spirit.

- We trust the Son to the same extent and with the same fervor that we trust the Father and the Holy Spirit.
- We thank the Holy Spirit to the same extent and with the same fervor that we thank the Father and the Son.

We worship and glorify our triune God: Father, Son, and Holy Spirit.

The first two truths lead to the third and final one.

Third, the Holy Spirit is fully God.

The creed refers to the Holy Spirit as "the Lord," which means He is God. In addition to this, He is "the Giver of Life," which means that, along with the Father and the Son, the Holy Spirit is the Creator of all creation and the Re-Creator of those who, by grace, are rescued from their sin and have become new creations. As Creator and Re-Creator, He is God. Moreover, together with God the Father and God the Son, the Holy Spirit is the object of worship and adoration, which further means He is God.

Of course, this truth reflects, and is supported by, biblical affirmations. For example, the narrative of Ananias and Sapphira recounts the sin of two early Christians. They attempted to deceive the church by offering a large amount of money as if it were the entirety of the proceeds from the sale of their land. The parallels in Peter's rebuke of Ananias underscore the deity of the Spirit:

> "Ananias," Peter asked, "why has Satan filled your heart to *lie to the Holy Spirit* and keep back part of the proceeds of the land? Wasn't it yours while you possessed it? And after it was sold, wasn't it at your disposal? Why is it that you planned this thing

in your heart? You have not *lied* to people but *to
God.*" (Acts 5:3–4)

Lying to the Holy Spirit is parallel to lying to God because the Holy
Spirit is fully God.

Peter's follow-up question to Sapphira is equally revealing:
"Why did you agree to test the Spirit of the Lord?" (5:9). In the Old
Testament, the expression "the Spirit of the Lord" refers to Yahweh,
the God of Israel, and putting God to the test was a severely pro-
hibited sin ("Do not test the LORD your God" [Deut. 6:16]). By
testing the Spirit of the Lord, this couple committed a serious sin
against the Holy Spirit, who is fully God.

Jesus underscored the Spirit's deity when He warned about
committing blasphemy against the Holy Spirit (Matt. 12:22–32).
Blasphemy is any speech that insults or shows contempt for God.
Moreover, only God can be blasphemed. Therefore, if the Holy
Spirit can be blasphemed, then He is God. This idea is echoed in a
warning in Hebrews: continuous, grievous sinning after hearing the
gospel leads to insulting the Spirit of grace, which results in divine
judgment (Heb. 10:29). Such condemnation is so because the Holy
Spirit is fully God.

The New Testament affirms the deity of the Holy Spirit when
it attributes the divine actions of Yahweh (recounted in the Old
Testament) to the Holy Spirit. For example, the transformation
from spiritual blindness to freely seeing the Lord is, in Exodus
34:29–35, ascribed to Yahweh. In 2 Corinthians 3:12–18, restoration of spiritual sight is ascribed to "the Lord who is the Spirit"
(v. 18). As another example, Jeremiah 31:31–34 attributes the
establishment of the new covenant to Yahweh, yet the writer to the
Hebrews (Heb. 10:15–18) attributes its establishment to the Holy

Spirit.[5] Divine actions of Yahweh are divine actions of the Holy Spirit, because the Holy Spirit is God.

Scripture also supports the Creed's confession that the Holy Spirit is "the Giver of Life," that is, the Creator. Commonly, we associate creation with the first person of the Trinity. God the Father is the one who spoke, and the universe and everything that it contains came into existence. For example, "God said, 'Let there be light,' and there was light" (Gen. 1:3). This truth leads us to affirm also that creation took place through the second person of the Trinity. That is, the Father spoke creation into existence through His Word, who is God the Son: "In the beginning was the Word, and the Word was with God, and the Word was God. He was with God in the beginning. All things were created through him, and apart from him not one thing was created that has been created" (John 1:1–3). Paul confirms the Son's active role in creation:

> Everything was created by him,
> in heaven and on earth,
> the visible and the invisible,
> whether thrones or dominions
> or rulers or authorities—
> all things have been created through him and for
>   him. (Col. 1:16; also Heb. 1:2)

The Father and the Son were engaged in the creation of heaven, earth, visible things, and invisible things.

But what of the third person and His role in creation? The Bible begins with an affirmation of the Spirit's creative work: "In the beginning God created the heavens and the earth. Now the

---

5. My thanks to Jacob Denhollander for pointing out this second example.

earth was formless and empty, darkness covered the surface of the watery depths, and the Spirit of God was hovering over the surface of the waters" (Gen. 1:1–2). The original state of the world as spoken by the Father through His Word, the Son, was formless (unstructured), empty (void of life), dark (pitch black so nothing could be seen), and watery (without a solid surface). To say the least, the original creation was unready to host living things, especially human beings. The role of the Spirit—the one "hovering over" this undefined mass—was to ready it for the upcoming work of the six-day creation. As the Father spoke through His Word, the Spirit spurred on the raw materials to respond obediently to the creation commands. So, for example, "God said, 'Let the water under the sky be gathered into one place, and let the dry land appear.' And it was so" (Gen. 1:9). The water was gathered, and the land appeared, by God's spoken Word and prepared by the Spirit of God to carry out His will for creation.[6]

As "the Lord and Giver of Life," the Spirit is fully God.

The Holy Spirit is Creator. He is to be worshipped and glorified together with the Father and the Son (who are divine persons). He spoke by the prophets. These truths that the church confesses imply that the Holy Spirit is a divine person, not a power, a force, or an influence. The same can be concluded by considering the personal characteristics exhibited by the Spirit:

> *intelligence:* He knows all things, including the depths of God and the future (1 Cor. 2:10–11; John 16:13)

> *emotions:* the Spirit can be grieved (Eph. 4:30)

---

6. For support for this role of the Holy Spirit in the original creation, see my fuller discussion in Allison and Köstenberger, *The Holy Spirit*, 296–301.

will: the Spirit sovereignly distributes spiritual gifts to church members (1 Cor. 12:11)

Additionally, the activities in which the Holy Spirit engages— teaching (John 14:26), praying (Rom. 8:26–27), speaking (John 16:13), bearing witness (John 15:26)—point to His person- hood. A power doesn't teach. A force doesn't pray. An influence doesn't speak. A vigor doesn't bear witness.

The Holy Spirit is a divine person, fully God.

This calls for some reflection time, both personal and in terms of your church.

> A power doesn't teach. A force doesn't pray. An influence doesn't speak. A vigor doesn't bear witness. The Holy Spirit is a divine person, fully God.

1. The co-eminence of the third person with the first person and the second person means that the praise, honor, adoration, obedience, trust, and thanksgiving that we direct to the Spirit does not differ in essence from those same activities directed toward the Father and the Son. Have you ever thought about the Holy Spirit in this way? If yes, what has encouraged you to do so? If no, what has hindered you from doing so?

2. If worship, honor, and adoration are due him, do you pray to the Holy Spirit? Why or why not? To help you answer this question, think about prayers you might direct toward the

Father. For example, "Thank You, Father, for sending Your Son, Jesus Christ, to die on the cross and to rise again so that I might be forgiven and have eternal life." You would *not* pray (at least I hope you wouldn't!), "Thank You, Father, for dying on the cross and rising again so that I might be forgiven and have eternal life." It was not the Father who did the work of salvation. That would be an example of a prayer you might direct toward the Son: "Thank You, Jesus Christ, Son of God, for Your death and resurrection."

Following this line of thinking, can you articulate a prayer you might direct toward the Holy Spirit? An example could be while sharing the gospel with an unbelieving friend, you pray, "Holy Spirit, please convict Meredith of her sin so that she realizes her need for Jesus" (developed from John 16:8–11). Another example could be before the reading and preaching of Scripture during a worship service, the pastor prays, "Holy Spirit, who inspired Scripture, please illumine Your Word so that we might rightly interpret it and, understanding it, might concretely apply it to our lives" (developed from Ps. 119:105; 1 Cor. 2:10–16). Agree or disagree?

3. How is your church doing in regard to worshipping, honoring, adoring, obeying, trusting, and thanking the Holy Spirit? What

elements in its worship services prompt church members to worship Him? What aspects of its discipleship endeavors, Sunday school and equipping classes, and mentoring relationships help to form members in knowledge of, love for, and submission to the Holy Spirit? What would you like to see continue or change in this regard?

CHAPTER 4

The Holy Spirit and the Holy Trinity

You may be wondering at this point how the Holy Spirit is different from God the Father and God the Son. We have been emphasizing the common nature of the three persons, explaining there is no distinction in terms of their divine attributes of all-powerfulness, love, holiness, unchangeableness, and the like. And we have affirmed with the early creeds that the Father, Son, and Holy Spirit are together to be worshipped and glorified.

So, how are there three persons? How do we distinguish between the Father, the Son, and the Holy Spirit? Specifically, for our purposes, how is the Spirit different from the other two divine persons?

Let me take a brief detour and offer a basic primer on the Trinity. (Warning: this topic is the deepest and most difficult doctrine there is, so don't despair if it takes you a few passes through this material!) By the end of the chapter, you'll see the payoff: how God the Holy Spirit engages in a mission to rescue us from sin and death. Beautifully, His mission is linked to the mission of God the

Son incarnate, and together they bring us back to God the Father—
that God may be all in all!

There are seven points in our primer:[1]

1. There was never time in which God did not exist.

Ø

(This mathematical sign represents the null set,
which means there are no examples in the set.)

2. There was never a time in which there existed a
generic god.

god

(The small "g" god symbolizes a nonspecific
divine being.)

3. There was never a time in which God was only
the Father.

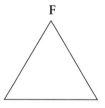

(The equilateral triangle is a standard representation of the Trinity. F stands for the Father.)

---

1. These ideas are developed in Gregg R. Allison and Andreas J.
Köstenberger, *The Holy Spirit: Theology for the People of God* (Nashville: B&H
Academic, 2020), 255–64.

4. There was never a time in which God was only the Father and the Son.

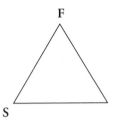

(The equilateral triangle is a standard representation of the Trinity. F stands for the Father and S stands for the Son.)

5. There was never a time in which God was *not* the Father, the Son, and the Holy Spirit.

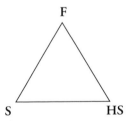

(The equilateral triangle is a standard representation of the Trinity. F stands for the Father, S stands for the Son, and HS stands for the Holy Spirit.)

6. God eternally exists as the Father, the Son, and the Holy Spirit.

7. So how are the three persons distinct? (Here's where we take a deep dive.) The three persons differ according to their eternal relations.[2]

Specifically, there are two relations of the triune God: these are called *relations of origin* (we'll see the reason for this name shortly) or *processions*.

The first procession is the relation of the Father and the Son. This is called *eternal generation* (or *eternal begottenness*). Put very simply, there has forever been a unique, special relationship— EG—between the Father and the Son.

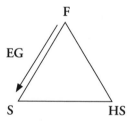

The second procession is the relation of the Father and the Son with the Holy Spirit; this is called *eternal procession* (or *eternal spiration*).[3] Put very

---

2. The distinction in eternal relations is one of two ways of distinguishing between the three persons. The distinction in roles with respect to creation, providence, salvation, and other divine works is the second way. It will not be discussed in this book, which concentrates on the works of the Holy Spirit.

3. *Spiration* has the idea of breathing. You will note that the word *procession* is used in two different ways. *Procession* in the first sense refers to both the eternal generation of the Son and the eternal procession of the Holy Spirit. *Procession* in the second sense refers only to the eternal procession of the Holy Spirit. The language of "procession" comes from Jesus's teaching about the Holy Spirit: "When the Counselor comes, the one I will send to you from

simply, there has forever been a unique, special relationship—EP—between the Father and the Son, and the Holy Spirit.

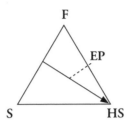

These two processions distinguish the three persons of the Trinity within the triune God Himself:

- Procession 1: the Father and the Son
- Procession 2: the Father and the Son, and the Holy Spirit

You will note there is no procession in regard to the Father: He is not eternally generated. He does not eternally proceed. This is due to the Father being first in order, the source of the two processions. Indeed, the eternal characteristic that is unique to the Father is *paternity*. As the first person in relation to the second person, He is eternally *the Father* of the Son.

As the source of the eternal processions, the Father is the originator of the processions. Thus, the processions are also called "relations of *origin*."

The first procession—*eternal generation*—is the relation of origin with respect to the Father and the Son. The eternal characteristic that is unique to the Son is *generation*. The first person eternally

---

the Father—the Spirit of truth who *proceeds* from the Father—he will testify about me" (John 15:26).

generates the second person. This does not mean that the Father created the Son. The Son is not created by the Father. It does not mean that the Son borrows deity from the Father. The Father does not lend "godness" to the Son. Rather, it means that the first person eternally grants the second person His person-of-the-divine-Son. He is *the Son* of the Father.

The second procession—*eternal procession*—is the relation of origin with respect to the Father and the Son, and the Holy Spirit. The eternal characteristic that is unique to the Holy Spirit is *procession*. The third person eternally proceeds from the first person and the second person. This does not mean that the Father and the Son created the Holy Spirit. The Holy Spirit is not created by the Father and the Son. The Holy Spirit does not borrow deity from the Father and the Son. The Father and the Son do not lend "godness" to the Spirit. Rather, it means that the first person and second person eternally grant the third person His person-of-the-divine-Spirit. The Holy Spirit *proceeds* from the Father and the Son.

I can hear an objection: This is SO deep and hard! Why do we bother talking about it? The simple answer is: the Bible affirms these deep truths about our triune God.

Where?!

Let's first look at the biblical basis for the first procession. Because this book is about the Holy Spirit, our attention will be limited to two key passages about the eternal generation of the Son from the Father. Speaking of His Father, Jesus states, "For as the Father has life in himself, so he *has granted the Son also to have life in himself*" (John 5:26 ESV). The church has historically understood Jesus's affirmation to refer to the first person's eternal "granting" of sonship life to the second person: the Father's eternal generation of the Son. The apostle John approaches it this way: "We know that *everyone who has been born of God* does not keep on sinning, but he *who was born of God* protects him, and the evil one does not touch him" (1 John 5:18 ESV). The first phrase "everyone who has been born of God" refers to us Christians who have been *regenerated* by the Holy Spirit. The second phrase "he who was born of God" refers to the second person: the Son who is *eternally generated* of the Father.

We may be tempted to understand John's reference to the Son as the one "who was born of God" in terms of human birth: what did not exist before comes into existence through birth in time and space. For example, my three children were "born of Nora" my wife/their mother. But that's not the way John intends us to understand the Son "who was born of God." This "birth" did not bring the Son, who did not exist, into existence. And it did not take place in time and space. Rather, the Son "was born of God" in the sense presented above: the Father, who is the first person, eternally grants the second person His person-of-the-divine-Son. Not birth in the sense of human birth. But "birth" in a divine sense of always being the Father of the always existing Son, who is eternally generated of the Father.

Second, let's turn to the biblical basis for the second procession, with greater attention to this topic. Three times in His Upper Room Discourse (John 13–17), Jesus comforts His disciples with important teaching about the Holy Spirit:

> "The Counselor, the Holy Spirit, whom *the Father will send in my name*, will teach you all things and remind you of everything I have told you." (14:26)

> "When the Counselor comes, the one *I will send to you from the Father*—the Spirit of truth *who*

proceeds from the Father—he will testify about me." (15:26)

"It is for your benefit that I go away, because if I don't go away the Counselor will not come to you. If I go, *I will send him to you.*" (16:7)

To summarize: The Father will send the Holy Spirit in Jesus's name. Jesus will send the Holy Spirit from the Father. Jesus will send the Holy Spirit.

To what event was Jesus referring when He promised that He and the Father would send the Holy Spirit? The day of Pentecost, which would occur a little over fifty days from when Jesus presented His teaching about the sending of the Spirit on that day. The apostle Peter confirms our understanding. In his gospel message on the day of Pentecost, Peter spoke about Jesus and explained the mighty outpouring of the Holy Spirit:

"God has raised this Jesus; we are all witnesses of this. Therefore, since he has been exalted to the right hand of God and has received from the Father the promised Holy Spirit, he has poured out what you both see and hear." (Acts 2:32–33)

From the Father, the Son has poured out the promised Holy Spirit on Pentecost. But why did the Father and the Son get to send the Holy Spirit on that day? The church's answer to this perceptive question is the eternal procession of the Holy Spirit. Because the first person and the second person eternally grant the third person His person-of-the-divine-Spirit, it was fitting that the Father and the Son would send the Holy Spirit in space and time, that is, on the day of Pentecost about two thousand years ago. The temporal sending of the Holy Spirit by the Father and the Son beautifully mirrors the eternal procession of the Spirit from the Father and the Son.

Unsurprisingly, then, the apostle Paul gives instructions to us related to the Holy Spirit: "You are not in the flesh, but in the Spirit, if indeed *the Spirit of God* lives in you. If anyone does not have *the Spirit of Christ*, he does not belong to him" (Rom. 8:9). The Holy Spirit is the *Spirit of God* who, in this context, is the Father. The Holy Spirit is the *Spirit of Christ*, who is the Son. He is the Spirit of the Father and of the Son, which is exactly what the eternal procession of the Holy Spirit affirms. He proceeds from the Father and the Son.

But what are we to make of Jesus's statement (which we've skipped until now) about "the Spirit of truth who *proceeds from the Father*" (John 15:26)? Jesus seems to affirm the eternal procession of the Spirit from the first person, not the first and second person (Himself). Importantly, Jesus did not say "the Spirit of truth who proceeds from the Father *alone*." Noting the absence of this limitation and putting together the rest of the Bible's teaching about the relations of the three persons, the church early on concluded (as we see in the Creed) "the Holy Spirit proceeds from the Father *and the Son*." This creedal confession does not contradict Jesus's statement, but simply adds to it on the basis of other biblical affirmations.[4]

To summarize the eternal distinctions of the three persons of the triune God:

---

4. After all, every verse in Scripture doesn't have to say everything there is to say on a particular topic.

- the Father is characterized by *paternity* in relationship to the Son: He is the Father of the Son
- the Son is characterized by *eternal generation* from the Father: He is the Son of the Father, eternally generated from the Father (Procession 1)
- the Holy Spirit is characterized by *eternal procession* from the Father and the Son: He eternally proceeds from the Father and the Son (Procession 2)

The importance of these two processions lies not only in helping us to know how the three persons differ. They also help us to understand the two missions of the triune God (here is the promised payoff of our difficult discussion).[5]

From these eternal processions flow the temporal missions of the Son and the Holy Spirit. A mission is a divine operation that takes place in our created world for our sake. The Son's mission—mission 1—is about incarnation and the work of accomplishing our salvation. The Spirit's mission—mission 2—is about being poured out on Pentecost and the work of applying salvation to our lives.

Importantly, we should not think in terms of processions and missions as separate matters. Rather, processions and missions are intimately connected: a mission is a procession turned outside and in time for the benefit of us image-bearers who have fallen into sin.[6]

---

5. For further discussion, see Allison and Köstenberger, *The Holy Spirit*, 273–86.

6. The following is adapted from Allison and Köstenberger, *The Holy Spirit*, 276.

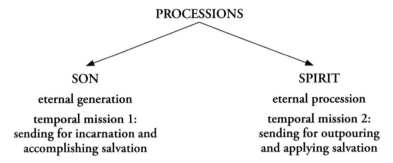

The temporal missions of the Son and the Spirit express and are reflective of their eternal processions. There is an appropriateness to the Son becoming incarnate and doing the work of accomplishing salvation as the particular mission 1 of the Son who is eternally generated by the Father. And there is an appropriateness to the Holy Spirit being poured out and doing the work of applying salvation as the particular mission 2 of the Holy Spirit who eternally proceeds from the Father and the Son.

So closely related are these two missions that we could also talk about one mission with two aspects. This interconnection will become especially clear and important when we talk later about salvation: our salvation from sin and progress in holiness is established by both the Son and the Spirit. Similarly, this interconnection will come to the forefront when we later address the church: the church is established by both the Son and the Spirit.[7] The missions of these two are so intertwined that they cannot be separated. So, we could say there is one mission of God with two aspects. And most important for us, the Son who is eternally generated from the Father, and the Spirit who eternally proceeds from the Father and the Son, undertake their missions on behalf of us image-bearers who have

---

7. We know this point through two biblical images for it: the church is both the body of Christ and the temple of the Holy Spirit. See chapter 11.

fallen into sin. Together through their missions, they save us and bring us back to our triune God.

You may be wondering, *Does anyone ever understand this stuff?* Believe it or not, they do!

A couple of years ago I was asked to teach the Trinity to a Sunday school class of fourth- and fifth-graders. I wondered—and worried!—whether any nine-year-old was going to understand what I would share with the class.

I started out by wearing a T-shirt with a diagram of the Trinity on it.

As soon as the class saw my shirt, they asked, "Are we going to learn about the Trinity?" I had their interest piqued!

Because trying to explain the diagram on my shirt while wearing it was too difficult, I drew the Trinity triangle on the whiteboard:

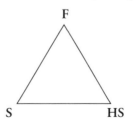

I next drew an ellipse around the F and the S, explaining that the Father and the Son have always had a special relationship.

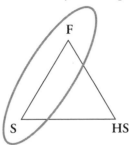

Much to my pleasant surprise, one ten-year-old blurted out, "Is that why God sent His only Son to die on the cross for our sins?" Jumping for joy (at least on the inside), I enthusiastically congratulated her! As the others nodded in agreement, I sensed we were making good progress.

The next question quickly brought me back down to earth: "What about that third dude on the right?" As the question came from a nine-year-old, I didn't take the reference to the Holy Spirit to be disrespectful or blasphemous. Besides, the questioner appeared to really want to know the answer to his question. So I drew a second ellipse, explaining that the Father with the Son, and the Holy Spirit, have always had a special relationship:

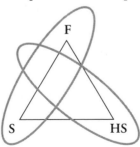

Intrigued but not quite satisfied, my still enthusiastic but now silent audience needed a prompt. So I asked them, "Where in our church do we see these three together?" One hand shot up: "We baptize people in the name of the Father and the Son and the Holy Spirit." Another reply quickly followed: "Right before we finish church, the pastor says, 'Go now in the name of the Father and the Son and the Holy Spirit. Peace be with you.'"

I was amazed!

Everyone was smiling—they had figured it out! My explanation that the third dude was poured out on the day of Pentecost didn't gain any traction with the kids. But that was okay. As fourth- and fifth-graders, they had learned the basics of the Trinity.

I hope you have too!

Ready for some questions for reflection?

1. Does this discussion help you to (better) understand the Trinity? What new truths did you learn? What questions do you still have? If you're (a bit) overwhelmed by this material, don't panic or despair! Reread this chapter and see if you gain (some) clarity.

2. Does this presentation help you make sense of why the Father sent the Son to become incarnate and accomplish the work of salvation? Does it help you to understand why the Father and the Son poured out the Holy Spirit on the day of Pentecost to carry on the ministry of the Son? Do you see how the two missions of the Son and the Spirit are intimately connected?

3. Does this chapter shed any light on Jesus's promise: "It is for your benefit that I go away, because if I don't go away the Counselor [the Holy Spirit] will not come to you. If I go, I will send him to you" (John 16:7)? In light of the eternal processions and temporal missions of the Son and the Spirit, why is Jesus's promise both true and necessary?

God's new
relationship
with His people
—the new covenant—
would feature a fresh,
unprecedented outpouring
of the Holy Spirit.

The Spirit's Divine Works

The last chapter explained that the distinction in eternal relations is one of two ways of distinguishing between the three persons of the Trinity. The distinction in roles with respect to creation, providence, salvation, and other divine works is the second way. Rather than focus on these distinctions, the following chapters concentrate on the works of the Holy Spirit. These are His works of speaking, conviction, salvation (two chapters), illumination and intercession, His works in the church, and perfection. Also included is a chapter on Jesus Christ's work of baptizing with the Holy Spirit. Though this mighty act of God is not the work of the Spirit, it does involve Him.

CHAPTER 5

The Holy Spirit's Work of Speaking

The Holy Spirit engages in the particular work of speaking.[1] Often in Scripture, when the Holy Spirit falls upon people, they engage in some kind of speech: praise, prophecy, prayer, or preaching. Consider a few examples, beginning with the Old Testament:

The seventy elders with Moses, along with two others, prophesied:

> [The Lord] took some of the Spirit who was on Moses and placed the Spirit on the seventy elders. *As the Spirit rested on them, they prophesied,* but they never did it again. Two men had remained in the camp, one named Eldad and the other Medad; *the Spirit rested on them*—they were among those

---

1. This section is adapted from Gregg R. Allison and Andreas J. Köstenberger, *The Holy Spirit: Theology for the People of God* (Nashville: B&H Academic, 2020), 286–89.

listed, but had not gone out to the tent—*and they prophesied* in the camp. (Num. 11:25–26)

King Saul prophesied:

When Saul and his servant arrived at Gibeah, a group of prophets met him. Then *the Spirit of God came powerfully on him, and he prophesied* along with them. Everyone who knew him previously and saw him *prophesy* with the prophets asked each other, "What has happened to the son of Kish? Is Saul also among the prophets?" Then a man who was from there asked, "And who is their father?" As a result, "Is Saul also among the prophets?" became a popular saying. Then *Saul finished prophesying* and went to the high place. (1 Sam. 10:10–13)

Some examples from the New Testament:
Elizabeth pronounced a blessing:

When Elizabeth heard Mary's greeting, the baby leaped inside her, and Elizabeth was *filled with the Holy Spirit.* Then *she exclaimed with a loud cry,* "Blessed are you among women, and your child will be blessed!" (Luke 1:41–42)

Zechariah praised the Lord:

Zechariah was *filled with the Holy Spirit* and *prophesied*: "Blessed is the Lord, the God of Israel, because he has visited and provided redemption for his people." (Luke 1:67–68)

The disciples spoke in tongues, declaring God's mighty works:

> "They were all *filled with the Holy Spirit* and began
> to *speak in different tongues*, as *the Spirit enabled
> them*" (Acts 2:4), and the audience heard the dis-
> ciples "*declaring* the magnificent acts of God" in
> the listeners' own tongues (v. 11).

The persecuted church proclaimed the gospel:

> When they had prayed, the place where they were
> assembled was shaken, and *they were all filled with
> the Holy Spirit* and began to *speak the word of God
> boldly*. (Acts 4:31)

Cornelius and his family and friends spoke in tongues, praising
God:

> While Peter was still speaking these words, *the
> Holy Spirit came down* on all those who heard
> the message. The circumcised believers who had
> come with Peter were amazed because the gift of
> *the Holy Spirit had been poured out* even on the
> Gentiles. For they heard them *speaking in tongues
> and declaring the greatness of God*. (Acts 10:44–46)

Paul rebuked a sorcerer and prophesied his demise:

> But Saul—also called Paul—*filled with the Holy
> Spirit*, stared straight at Elymas and *said*, "You
> are full of all kinds of deceit and trickery, you son
> of the devil and enemy of all that is right. Won't
> you ever stop perverting the straight paths of the
> Lord? Now, look, the Lord's hand is against you.

> *You are going to be blind,* and will not see the sun
> for a time." Immediately a mist and darkness fell
> on him, and he went around seeking someone to
> lead him by the hand. (Acts 13:9–11)

The twelve disciples of John the Baptist spoke in tongues and prophesied:

> When they heard this, they were baptized into the
> name of the Lord Jesus. And when Paul had laid
> his hands on them, *the Holy Spirit came on them,*
> and they began *to speak in tongues and to prophesy.*
> (Acts 19:5–6)

The apostle John, *speaking "in the Spirit"* (Rev. 1:10), addressed the seven churches, concluding with the same exhortation to each group:

> "Let anyone who has ears to hear *listen to what the
> Spirit says* to the churches." (Rev. 2:7, 11, 17, 29;
> 3:6, 13, 22)

These examples could be multiplied many times. They underscore the fact that one of the particular works of the Holy Spirit is speaking.

The last example (Rev. 2–3) reminds us that the Bible in its entirety is God's Word inspired by the Holy Spirit. "All Scripture is inspired [breathed out] by God" (2 Tim. 3:16–17); that is, Scripture is the communicative product of the creative breath of God. More specifically, "No prophecy of Scripture comes from the prophet's own interpretation, because no prophecy ever came by the will of man; instead, men spoke from God as they were carried along by the Holy Spirit" (2 Pet. 1:20–21). The origin of Scripture is divine.

It is not the product of human ingenuity, willpower, initiative, or interpretation. At the same time, Scripture is humanly written. The Holy Spirit superintended the biblical authors—Moses, David, Luke, Paul—at every step of their writing. What we have as a result is the divinely inspired, authoritative, truthful Word of God.[2]

To summarize, one of the particular works of the Holy Spirit is speaking. According to Scripture, when the Spirit fell/rushed/came/descended/rested upon people, filling them with

> Scripture is the communicative product of the creative breath of God.

His presence, they engaged in prophecy, prayer, praise, and proclamation. And Scripture itself is divine speech in written form, inspired by the Holy Spirit. He is the speaking God!

Time for some application.

1. How can you practically rely on the Holy Spirit as you approach the Bible to read and study it? As you give counsel to others? As you share the gospel? As you lead a Bible study?

2. How is your church doing in this regard? Where in the preaching, teaching, counseling, discipling, and other ministries of your church does reliance on the Holy Spirit's work of speaking become evident?

---

2. For further discussion on the Holy Spirit and Scripture, see Allison and Köstenberger, *The Holy Spirit*, 307–23.

CHAPTER 6

The Holy Spirit's Work of Conviction

Even before people embrace the gospel, the Holy Spirit is at work to "convict the world about sin, righteousness, and judgment" (John 16:8).[1] In John's Gospel, *convict* means to expose guilt due to sin and the condemnation that results from it. Moreover, "the world" refers to people who are hostile toward God. They are not in a good place before God. They aren't even in a neutral space. On the contrary, they are in dire straits before God; they are guilty because of their sin and stand under God's condemnation. Tragically, many are not even aware of their plight. They don't understand that they're in grave danger. And before they can embrace the good news of God's grace in Christ, they must grasp the bad news that they are sinners before a holy God.

---

1. This section is adapted from Gregg R. Allison and Andreas J. Köstenberger, *The Holy Spirit: Theology for the People of God* (Nashville: B&H Academic, 2020), 340–43.

Here is where the Holy Spirit's ministry of conviction enters in. He convicts unaware people of three major faults: sin, righteousness, and judgment. Let's take each fault in turn.[2] First, in Jesus's words, the Holy Spirit convicts "about sin, because they do not believe in me" (16:9). John's Gospel may be called the *Gospel of Belief*; it sets forth who Jesus is and how to believe in Him for eternal life.[3] John himself explains his method of selecting which stories to tell about Jesus, "these are written so *that you may believe* that Jesus is the Messiah, the Son of God, and *that by believing* you may have life in his name" (20:31).

If John's Gospel is all about belief, then the ultimate sin is unbelief. Graciously and thankfully, the Holy Spirit operates to shake people out of their doldrums—inattention to their precarious state, indifference toward God and His provision of salvation—and underscores that they have not yet believed in Jesus Christ. And He is the only way for them to be saved (John 14:6). This conviction readies them for the good news.

Second, in Jesus's words, the Spirit convicts people "about righteousness, because I am going to the Father and you will no longer see me" (16:10). Importantly, "righteousness" is a good, desirable characteristic, but John's discussion about the convicting work of the Holy Spirit is not about good things. "Self-righteousness," however, is a futile, wrongheaded approach to gaining God's favor. In this context, it qualifies as a fault for which the Holy Spirit brings conviction.

---

2. My interpretation relies on Carson's discussion in D. A. Carson, *The Gospel According to John* (Leicester, UK: InterVarsity, 1991), 536–39.

3. For example, Merrill C. Tenney's commentary on the fourth Gospel is titled *John: The Gospel of Belief* (Grand Rapids: Eerdmans, 1997).

As John's Gospel emphasizes, many of Jesus's Jewish adversaries were very religious people. Specifically, they tried to establish their own righteousness by relying on four pillars:

1. *Trusting their Jewish ancestry;* as they claimed, "We are descendants of Abraham" (8:33). They relied on their pedigree to make them right before God.

2. *Observing the Sabbath:* "The Jews said to the man who had been healed [by Jesus], 'This is the Sabbath. The law prohibits you from picking up your mat'" (5:10). They so carefully practiced the laws of rest to earn God's approval that they would even try to prevent Jesus from healing on the Sabbath.

3. *Frequenting the temple:* "The Jews said [to Jesus], 'This temple took forty-six years to build, and will you raise it up in three days?'" (2:20). The temple was the center of their religious ceremonies, and they relied on regular attendance at it to merit God's favor.

4. *Possessing the Law of Moses;* as Jesus chided, "Do not think that I will accuse you to the Father. Your accuser is Moses, on whom you have set your hope" (5:45). They counted on the Law, but it actually accused them of engaging in a futile quest for righteousness.

In these and other cases, Jesus exposed the futility of relying on Jewish lineage, Sabbath-keeping, attending temple services, and having the Mosaic Law. But Jesus would soon be leaving this world, so would His work of exposing self-righteousness come to an end? No, because He would send the Holy Spirit to take over that convicting work. Graciously and thankfully, the Holy Spirit undercuts reliance on mere human attempts to merit the love and forgiveness of God. Tearing down the scaffolding of self-righteousness, the Spirit collapses those futile ways of trying to return to God. This conviction readies people for the good news.

Third, in Jesus's words, the Holy Spirit convicts people "about judgment, because the ruler of this world has been judged" (16:11). Interestingly, "judgment" can be both a good thing and an evil thing. "Good judgment" involves wisdom and astuteness in rightly evaluating people and situations. But the convicting work of the Holy Spirit according to John's Gospel is not about good things. "Worldly judgment" is a flawed, deficient evaluation of people and circumstances. In this context, it qualifies as a fault for which the Holy Spirit brings conviction.

> Graciously and thankfully, the Holy Spirit undercuts reliance on mere human attempts to merit the love and forgiveness of God.

John's Gospel itself contrasts these two kinds of judgment. On the one hand, Jesus's judgment is always right and true (7:24; 8:16). On the other hand, the world's judgment is carnal, superficial, and mistaken. It is an evaluation based on beauty and handsomeness, wealth and possessions, comfort and security, fame and influence, power and control. Jesus Himself condemned it: "Stop judging according to outward appearances; rather judge according to righteous judgment" (7:24). Such worldly judgment stems from

Satan—"the ruler of this world"—who has been judged by the victorious crucified Jesus (12:31). Graciously and thankfully, the Holy Spirit condemns such faulty, Satan-influenced judgment. This conviction readies people for the good news.

I became a Christian my senior year in high school. I vividly recall hearing the testimony of a guy my same age—I'll call him Zeke—who shared about his personal relationship with God. I had never heard of such a thing, but I was intrigued. Zeke had been a drug addict, yet his entire life had been radically changed by a miraculous encounter with Jesus Christ. Hearing his testimony, most people were happy and thankful for God's intervention in Zeke's life. But I was not impressed at all. My sentiments were just the opposite; Zeke was a loser. Of course, he needed Jesus. I considered myself a good kid: I believed in God, got good grades in school, stayed out of trouble, obeyed my parents, attended church, even served as a leader in the youth group. I had clearly merited God's love and favor. By my assessment, I was much, much better than Zeke.

With my head full of these off-base thoughts, I experienced the convicting work of the Holy Spirit. He revealed to me that I had never believed in Jesus, specifically His death and resurrection for my salvation from sin. The Spirit helped me to see that I was futilely relying on my own good deeds. I was full of self-righteousness, which was no way to come to God. The Holy Spirit exposed my faulty assessment; I had measured myself against Zeke the drug addict, so my worldly judgment was that I was far superior to him.

I was undone. The Holy Spirit's conviction was clear and unyielding.

I did the only thing I knew to do: I cried out, "God save me!" And He did!

Of course, this convicting work of the Holy Spirit does not stop once we become followers of Jesus. For example, as we read Scripture, we hear a rebuke like "do not lie to one another" (Col. 3:9). The Spirit confronts us with our terrible habit of stretching the truth to make ourselves seem more than we really are. So we alter how we speak about ourselves. Or we hear a sermon on Jesus's challenge to love our enemies (Matt. 5:44). The Spirit exposes our pattern of rejecting those who dislike us or mock us for our faith. So we change our relationship with them. Graciously and thankfully, the Holy Spirit convicts us deliberately, patiently, lovingly, and correctively. This conviction furthers our sanctification, or progress in becoming more like Jesus.

Some questions for reflection:

1. When you heard the gospel, what was your experience of the convicting work of the Holy Spirit?

2. In what areas is the Holy Spirit convicting you presently? How should you respond to Him?

3. Would you agree with this idea from Karl Barth?

Man, even the Christian man, is not aware that he is a sinner, particularly a sinner against God. Citing Martin Luther, Barth continued, "The name Comforter . . . means that the Holy Spirit must discharge his office at no place [except] where there is *no* comfort to be found and where comfort is needed and longed for. Therefore, [the Spirit] cannot comfort hard heads and haughty hearts, for they have never suffered flounderings or rejections." It is these sufferings that become— unexpectedly, in the Holy Spirit—saving graces:

"These very 'flounderings' and rejections, this
very lack of comfort when felt, are signs of the
Holy Spirit's work as Comforter."[4]

If this idea is correct, then my invitation is to welcome divinely
sent disturbances as promptings to know our sins and, therefore, to experience the Holy Spirit's helping work to confess
our sins and to receive God's forgiveness. What do you think?

4. As you share the gospel with your friends, how can you be
encouraged by the work of the Holy Spirit in convicting them
of sin, self-righteousness, and worldly judgment?

---

4. Adapted from Allison and Köstenberger, *The Holy Spirit*, 341–42. The
citations are from Karl Barth, *The Holy Spirit and the Christian Life* (Louisville,
KY: Westminster/John Knox, 1993), 29–33.

CHAPTER 7

The Holy Spirit's Work in Salvation (Part 1)

As the Holy Spirit's convicting work grips the hearts of unbelievers, He readies them to embrace the gospel of the salvation accomplished by Jesus Christ. This act of salvation actually encompasses many aspects. In this chapter, I focus on the initial mighty acts of the Holy Spirit at the start of our salvation. These mighty works are regeneration, conversion, union with Christ, justification, and adoption. In chapter 9, I will turn to the Spirit's ongoing works: sealing, sanctification, and assurance of salvation.

Regeneration

Paul describes the reception of the good news of Jesus Christ by the Thessalonians: "our gospel did not come to you in word only, but also in power, in the Holy Spirit, and with full assurance" (1 Thess. 1:5). The Word of God moves nonbelievers to be born again:

You have been born again—not of perishable
seed but of imperishable—through the living and
enduring word of God. For
    All flesh is like grass,
        and all its glory like a flower of the grass.
    The grass withers, and the flower falls,
        but the word of the Lord endures forever.
And this word is the gospel that was proclaimed
to you.
            (1 Pet. 1:23–25; citing Isa. 40:4, 8)

In concert with the Word of God proclaimed, the Spirit of God
effects regeneration.[1] This mighty act of God is the removal of the
old sinful nature and the implanting of a new nature. Gone is the
old self, the old life, the old identity that is typified by selfishness,
rebellion or indifference toward God, sinfulness, disregard for others, and the like. In its place is the new self, the new life, the new
identity that is expressed as Christ-centeredness, love for God, holiness, and love for others.

Jesus Himself taught that the Holy Spirit brings about regeneration: "Truly I tell you, unless someone is born of water and the
Spirit, he cannot enter the kingdom of God" (John 3:5). Jesus
underscores that entrance into the kingdom of God is through
the divine action of being born again. Earlier in this Gospel, John
had emphasized that those who believe the good news are "born,
not of natural descent, or of the will of the flesh, or of the will of
man, but of God" (John 1:13). Regeneration is no human activity.

---

1. For further discussion, see Gregg R. Allison and Andreas J. Köstenberger,
The Holy Spirit: Theology for the People of God (Nashville: B&H Academic,
2020), 369–74.

Unbelievers cannot cause themselves to become born again. Rather, Jesus insists, "unless someone is born of water and the Spirit," there is no salvation.

Let's not misunderstand Jesus's call to regeneration: (1) It does not mean that people must be baptized ("born of water" = water of baptism) and spiritually transformed ("born of . . . the Spirit"). (2) It does not mean that people must be physically born ("born of water" = the mother's amniotic fluid out of which a child is born) and spiritually born ("born of . . . the Spirit"). Rather, Jesus's call is about one thing, and it is a divine work that brings about the new birth.

In the background of Jesus's words is an Old Testament passage that prophesies a future outpouring of the Holy Spirit:

> "I will sprinkle clean water on you, and you will be clean. I will cleanse you from all your impurities and all your idols. I will give you a new heart and put a new spirit within you; I will remove your heart of stone and give you a heart of flesh. I will place my Spirit within you and cause you to follow my statutes and carefully observe my ordinances." (Ezek. 36:25–27)

In His conversation with Nicodemus, Jesus alludes to Ezekiel's prophecy. God's work of salvation will involve sprinkling with water—a vivid picture of cleansing from sin ("born of water")—together with the gift of a new heart/new spirit, indeed, the indwelling of the Spirit ("born of . . . Spirit"). Not two things—baptism plus the Spirit's renewal, or physical birth plus spiritual birth—but one thing: regeneration by the Holy Spirit.

Paul picks up on this theme:

> [God] saved us—not by works of righteousness
> that we had done, but according to his mercy—
> through the washing of regeneration and renewal
> by the Holy Spirit. He poured out his Spirit on
> us abundantly through Jesus Christ our Savior so
> that, having been justified by his grace, we may
> become heirs with the hope of eternal life. (Titus
> 3:5–7)

This "washing of regeneration" parallels Jesus's instructions about "being born of water and the Spirit." Regeneration involves cleansing from sin and the transformation of one's very nature. In Paul's words, "if anyone is in Christ, he is a new creation; the old has passed away, and see, the new has come!" (2 Cor. 5:17). Regeneration, or being born again, is the work of the Holy Spirit.

Conversion

As we just explained, regeneration is totally the work of God. It involves no human activity at all. At the same time, the Holy Spirit's work of regeneration is met by a corresponding human response: conversion, which features repentance from sin and faith in Jesus Christ, whom born-again people confess as their Lord.[2] All these aspects of conversion are closely linked to the work of the Holy Spirit.

Repentance is turning from sin. As discussed in the last chapter, the Spirit convicts people who are hostile toward God of their sin of unbelief, their futile reliance on their self-righteous efforts to return

---

2. For further discussion, see Allison and Köstenberger, *The Holy Spirit*, 379–83.

to God, and their faulty judgment. Being undone, Spirit-convicted people acknowledge that they are sinful and thus displeasing to God. They sense a deep sorrow for their sin. They willfully decide to break from sin by turning from it. This awakening of their consciousness of sin comes about through the Holy Spirit.

Faith is personal trust in Jesus Christ. With a consciousness of their sinfulness, people understand who Jesus is and what He has done to rescue them from their dreadful plight. They sense their deep need for forgiveness. They willfully decide to embrace salvation by trusting Jesus Christ to graciously save them. This faith to embrace the gracious salvation through Christ comes about through the Holy Spirit: "For you are saved by grace through faith, and this is not from yourselves; it is God's gift—not from works, so that no one can boast" (Eph. 2:8–9).

Following their conversion, new believers confess that Jesus is now their Lord:

> You know that when you were pagans, you used to
> be enticed and led astray by mute idols. Therefore
> I want you to know that no one speaking by the
> Spirit of God says, "Jesus is cursed," and no one
> can say, "Jesus is Lord," except by the Holy Spirit.
> (1 Cor. 12:2–3)

As presented earlier, when the Holy Spirit comes upon people, they engage in some kind of speech. In this case, those who turn from following idols—power, wealth, sex, comfort, security, the gods and goddesses of other religions—to following Christ, speak by the Holy Spirit. They confess "Jesus is Lord" and they are saved through Him.

Conversion and confession of Christ is aided by the work of the Holy Spirit.

Union with Christ

Being born again, repenting from sin, trusting in Christ by faith, and confessing Jesus is Lord signal that believers are united with Christ.[3] Paul addresses this work of the Holy Spirit:

> You are not in the flesh, but in the Spirit, if indeed *the Spirit of God lives in you.* If anyone does not have the Spirit of Christ, he does not belong to him. Now if *Christ is in you,* the body is dead because of sin, but the Spirit gives life because of righteousness. (Rom. 8:9–10)

The parallels are striking:

- "the Spirit of God lives in you"
- "Christ is in you"

Through the indwelling of the Holy Spirit, Jesus Christ Himself dwells in believers.

For Paul, the fact that Christ is in believers is part of a broader divine work: union with Christ. Through this union, believers are identified with Christ's death, burial, resurrection, and ascension (Rom. 6:1–11; Eph. 2:6). Thus, when God looks upon believers, He sees them as having died to sin, released from its power, raised to new life, and seated with Christ in heaven. What is true of Christ is true of believers as well!

Importantly, through union with Christ, believers receive all the benefits of salvation. As Paul notes, God the Father "has blessed

---

3. For further discussion, see Allison and Köstenberger, *The Holy Spirit,* 374.

us in Christ with every spiritual blessing in the heavenly places"
(Eph. 1:3). These gracious benefits include:

- election, that is, being chosen in Christ before
  the foundation of the world (v. 4)
- predestination for adoption as sons of God
  (v. 5)
- grace, that is, God's unmerited favor (v. 6;
  2 Tim. 1:9)
- redemption through the blood of Christ, that
  is, the forgiveness of sins (v. 7)
- knowledge of the mystery of God's will, that
  is, the summation of all things in Christ (v. 9)
- an inheritance (v. 11), which includes eternal
  life in the new heaven and new earth
- the sealing with "the promised Holy Spirit,
  who is the guarantee of our inheritance until
  we acquire possession of it" (v. 14)

Union with Christ is affected by the Holy Spirit, and through this
identification with Christ come all God's gracious blessings of
salvation.

Justification

Justification is the mighty work of God by which He declares
sinful people "not guilty" but "righteous instead."[4] Unlike regeneration, which is a transformative work that changes believers' very
nature, justification is a legal pronouncement: As judge, God enters

---

4. For further discussion, see Allison and Köstenberger, *The Holy Spirit*,
375–76.

a "not guilty" verdict for ungodly people. Even more, God declares them "righteous instead," not because they are righteous in and of themselves or because they have worked hard to earn a righteous status before God. Rather, God credits to their account the righteousness of Jesus Christ. Thus, as God sees believers, He sees them clothed in the righteousness of Christ. They are "not guilty" but "righteous instead."

> As God sees believers, He sees them clothed in the righteousness of Christ. They are "not guilty" but "righteous instead."

As hinted at above, justification is not according to works; that is, unbelievers cannot work hard—going to church, helping out others through good deeds, trying to act morally—so as to merit righteousness in God's sight. Paul is especially clear on this matter:

- We conclude that a person is justified by faith apart from the works of the law (Rom. 3:28).
- David speaks of the blessing of the person to whom God credits righteousness apart from works (Rom. 4:6).
- We know that a person is not justified by the works of the law but by faith in Jesus Christ (Gal. 2:16).

God does not declare sinful people "not guilty" but "righteous instead" because they engage in good works so as to earn His love and forgiveness. On the contrary, God's justification of Abraham becomes the model for Christians:

What then will we say that Abraham, our forefather according to the flesh, has found? If Abraham was justified by works, he has something to boast about—but not before God. For what does the Scripture say? "Abraham believed God, and it was credited to him for righteousness." Now to the one who works, pay is not credited as a gift, but as something owed. But to the one who does not work, but believes on him who justifies the ungodly, his faith is credited for righteousness. (Rom. 4:1–5)

Justification is by faith and faith alone. But how do sinful people have faith that they then express so as to be declared "not guilty" but "righteous instead"? Paul answers: "you were justified in the name of the Lord Jesus Christ and by the Spirit of our God" (1 Cor. 6:11). Justification is accomplished by the death and resurrection of Christ. And it is received by faith that comes from the Holy Spirit. The Spirit prompts the faith by which sinful people embrace justification and are thus declared "not guilty" but "righteous instead."[5] Justification comes about by the work of the Holy Spirit.

Adoption

Adoption is the mighty work of God by which He chooses sinful people to be incorporated into His family forever.[6] Their former

---

5. Galatians 3:2–6 associates the Holy Spirit, faith for believing God, and God's crediting righteousness to Abraham. Thus, while the word *justification* does not occur in this passage, it seems like it is further support for the view that the Spirit prompts the faith by which people are justified.

6. For further discussion, see Allison and Köstenberger, *The Holy Spirit*, 376–79.

status as enemies who were opposed to God and thus separated from Him is changed to the status of beloved children. While adoption involves Jesus Christ's work of redemption, the Holy Spirit operates as well: He is "the Spirit of adoption" (Rom. 8:15) by whom believers are brought into God's new family. Through the Spirit, the newly adopted children cry out, "*Abba*, Father!" to God (Gal. 4:4–6).

Justification is accomplished by the death and resurrection of Christ. And it is received by faith that comes from the Holy Spirit. The Spirit prompts the faith by which sinful people embrace justification and are thus declared "not guilty" but "righteous instead."

An important benefit of adoption is sonship. As Paul describes an adopted child: "you are no longer a slave but a son, and if a son, then God has made you an heir" (Gal. 4:4–7; Rom. 8:14–15). Why doesn't Paul use less sexist language and address both sons and daughters? He would seem more inclusive of both men and women whom God adopts.

In the Bible, "sonship" links up with inheritance. For example, it was customary in biblical times for the firstborn son to inherit the family's wealth and possessions. As the father of the family was dying, he would confer the family's inheritance upon the firstborn son. In other words, "sonship" was a status of family favor.

Paul's use of "sonship" picks up on this tradition, with an important twist: becoming "sons of God" means the adopted heirs receive divine favor and its gracious blessings. Even more, all the adopted heirs—not just the firstborn son, but all male and female believers—receive divine favor along with all its blessings of salvation. Again, for emphasis: adoption is true equally of women and men who enter the family of God the Father through the redemption of Christ and through the reception of "the Spirit of adoption." With this adoption comes the inheritance of divine favor, blessings that are conferred on both female Christians and male Christians alike. As Paul highlights:

> Through faith you are all sons of God in Christ Jesus. For those of you who were baptized into Christ have been clothed with Christ. There is no Jew or Greek, slave or free, male and female; since you are all one in Christ Jesus. And if you belong to Christ, then you are Abraham's seed, heirs according to the promise. (Gal. 3:26–29)

Being adopted into the family of God, women and men together receive the inheritance of divine blessing and are one in sharing those privileges.

Adoption takes place by the work of the Holy Spirit.

In conclusion:

regeneration

conversion

union with Christ

justification

adoption

These mighty works of God in which the Holy Spirit is active at the beginning of salvation invite some application.

1. Whether it was a long time ago or fairly recently, what do you recall of your being born again? Was it a dramatic event? Was it preceded by a long period of investigation and reflection? What was the message of the gospel that you heard and that led to your regeneration? What did repentance look like for you? How did you express your faith in Christ? What were the initial changes that the Holy Spirit operated in your life?

2. How has this chapter helped you understand the importance of being united with Christ for your life? How does water baptism vividly portray your union with Christ?

3. How does Paul's application point for justification encourage you? "There is now no condemnation for those who are in Christ Jesus" (Rom. 8:1)? How can God's mighty act of declaring you "not guilty" but "righteous instead" help you when you feel guilty and ashamed because of your sin?

4. Think about the cry "Abba, Father!" It's not some kind of rote prayer repeated as a chant to ward off evil. It's not some type of generic prayer to "the big guy upstairs." Rather, as a prayer prompted by "the Spirit of adoption," it is directed to our good, loving, and wise Father as an expression of our constant dependence on Him for all things. What does this prayer look like for you?

CHAPTER 8

Jesus Christ's Work of Baptizing with the Holy Spirit

Though all the other chapters in this section start with "The Holy Spirit's Work . . .", this chapter begins with "Jesus Christ's Work . . ." and addresses the Holy Spirit as the one with whom the Lord baptizes new believers.[1] This idea may sound strange, and the reason is at least twofold: First, most Christians and churches from a certain segment of Christianity rarely talk about baptism with the Spirit. By contrast, this near silence is not at all true of other segments of Christianity—Pentecostal churches and various charismatic movements. (If you're not familiar with these groups, don't worry; I'll talk about them shortly.) If you're part of the silent

---

1. For further discussion, see Gregg R. Allison and Andreas J. Köstenberger, *The Holy Spirit: Theology for the People of God* (Nashville: B&H Academic, 2020), 383–95.

segment, then it's no surprise that you've never considered baptism with the Holy Spirit—even though you've experienced it!

A second reason for the strangeness of this topic is due in part to the fears that the first segment has about the second segment. If you've ever attended a Pentecostal church or been part of a charismatic movement and had a bad experience, you'll probably try to stay as far away as possible from baptism with the Spirit. This distancing may be due to feeling pressure to speak in tongues to show that you've been baptized by the Spirit. Or it may be due to feeling like you're a second-class Christian if you've not experienced this Spirit baptism. Or your avoidance may be due to doubts about the legitimacy of prophecies and claims of miraculous healings. Whatever the reason may be, baptism with the Spirit is a tension point among Christians today.

I begin this chapter with a discussion of the experience of baptism with the Holy Spirit. Believe it or not—or heard of it or not—all Christians have been baptized with the Holy Spirit. Importantly, it is one of the most overlooked works of Jesus Christ as He saves us. After talking about this experience, I then present the debate over baptism with the Spirit.

> All Christians have been baptized with the Holy Spirit.

The Experience of Baptism with the Spirit

As John the Baptist carried out his ministry of baptism of repentance for the forgiveness of sin, he deflected the curiosity that he might be the Messiah. "I baptize you with water, but one who is more powerful than I am is coming. I am not worthy to untie the strap of his sandals. He will baptize you with the Holy Spirit and fire" (Luke 3:16; par. Matt. 3:11–12; Mark 1:7–8; John 1:26–27). The impending change that John the Baptist prophesied was from his baptism with water to the Messiah's baptism with the Holy Spirit. The apostle John added to the Baptist's prophecy, explaining that the Messiah would be "the one who baptizes with the Holy Spirit" (John 1:33). That is, one of the ongoing ministries of the Messiah would be that of pouring out the Holy Spirit upon His followers. In other words, the Messiah would inundate His disciples with the Spirit!

This promise of John the Baptist had a long tradition with the people of Israel. The prophet Jeremiah had prophesied:

> "Look, the days are coming"—this is the LORD's declaration—"when I will make a new covenant with the house of Israel and with the house of Judah. This one will not be like the covenant I made with their ancestors on the day I took them by the hand to lead them out of the land of Egypt—my covenant that they broke even though I am their master"—the LORD's declaration. "Instead, this is the covenant I will make with the house of Israel after those days"—the LORD's declaration. "I will put my teaching within them and write it on their hearts. I will be their God, and they will be my people. No longer will one teach his neighbor or his brother, saying, 'Know the LORD,' for they will all know me, from the least to the greatest of them"—this is the LORD's declaration. "For I will forgive their iniquity and never again remember their sin." (Jer. 31:31–34)

Jeremiah had predicted the cessation of the old or Mosaic covenant and its replacement with a new covenant. This new relationship that God would establish with His people would contain an ability for them to keep the covenant (unlike they did with the earlier covenant). It would introduce an interiority of the law; God's moral will would be written on their hearts. This new covenant would include all of God's people, because all of them would know the Lord personally. Finally, it would feature the complete forgiveness of sins.

A bit later, the prophet Ezekiel picked up on Jeremiah's prophecy, giving more detail:

> "I will sprinkle clean water on you, and you will be clean. I will cleanse you from all your impurities and all your idols. I will give you a new heart and put a new spirit within you; I will remove your heart of stone and give you a heart of flesh. I will place my Spirit within you and cause you to follow my statutes and carefully observe my ordinances." (Ezek. 36:25–27)

Like Jeremiah's promise, Ezekiel's prophecy included the forgiveness of sins. It used the image of sprinkled water; as a cleansing agent, it washes what is dirty and renders it clean. Similarly, God's new relationship with His people would feature a purification from all impurities. Ezekiel's promise included an interior renewal; God's people would be characterized by a new, soft heart in place of an old, stony heart. Important for our purposes, this prophecy added a new work of God: He would put the Holy Spirit within His people. Being indwelt with the Spirit, they would be able to obey His moral law and please Him.

The prophet Joel advanced these two prophecies:

> After this
> I will pour out my Spirit on all humanity;
> then your sons and your daughters will prophesy,
> your old men will have dreams,
> and your young men will see visions.
> I will even pour out my Spirit
> on the male and female slaves in those days.
> (Joel 2:28–29)

Joel's phrase "in those days" would be shaped by Peter on the day of Pentecost when he cited this prophecy: "in those days" would refer to "in the last days." This period, stretches from the Messiah's first coming—the incarnation of the Son as the God-man, Jesus of Nazareth—to the second coming of Christ. Remarkably, this era would be the age of the Spirit, who would be poured on all of God's people—men and women, old and young, slave and free.

To summarize this prophetic preparation, God's new relationship with His people—the new covenant—would feature a fresh, unprecedented outpouring of the Holy Spirit. And the people of Israel lived with the expectation of the fulfillment of this promise.

It fell to John the Baptist to announce the beginning of this fulfillment. The Messiah would

> God's new relationship with His people—the new covenant—would feature a fresh, unprecedented outpouring of the Holy Spirit. And the people of Israel lived with the expectation of the fulfillment of this promise.

baptize God's people with the Holy Spirit. Though John did not realize it as he was speaking, the Messiah was already in his midst: Jesus, God the Son incarnate. From all eternity, the Son was with the Holy Spirit.[2] From the moment of His conception as the God-man, He was filled with the Holy Spirit "without measure" (John 3:34).

Like Jeremiah, Ezekiel, Joel, and John the Baptist before Him, Jesus continued and heightened the expectation of a fresh, unprecedented outpouring of the Holy Spirit:

> On the last and most important day of the festival, Jesus stood up and cried out, "If anyone is thirsty, let him come to me and drink. The one who believes in me, as the Scripture has said, will have streams of living water flow from deep within him." He said this about the Spirit. Those who believed in Jesus were going to receive the Spirit, for the Spirit had not yet been given because Jesus had not yet been glorified. (John 7:37–39)

From Jesus's perspective, the fulfillment of the prophecy of the outpouring of the Spirit was still a future hope. It awaited His death, burial, resurrection, and ascension—the events of Jesus's glorification. After those events, by which He would accomplish salvation for His followers, Jesus would pour out the Spirit. As a result, His disciples would experience the Spirit's fullness like a flowing stream of life-giving water.

Before He embarked on His march to the cross, Jesus comforted His disciples:

---

2. See the earlier discussion (chap. 4) on the Trinity and the relationship of the Son and the Holy Spirit.

"I will ask the Father, and he will give you another Helper, to be with you forever, even the Spirit of truth, whom the world cannot receive, because it neither sees him nor knows him. You know him, for he dwells with you and will be in you." (John 14:16–17 ESV)

Certainly, Jesus's disciples were not unfamiliar with the Holy Spirit. He was not a stranger. On the contrary, the Spirit was with them and dwelt with them. But a change was about to happen. The Spirit would not merely *dwell with* Jesus's disciples. He would *dwell in* them. Jesus extended and expanded the long-awaited promise of a fresh, unprecedented outpouring of the Holy Spirit.

Giving instructions to His disciples after His crucifixion and resurrection, Jesus told them to wait for this promised event—or, better, promised person: "Look, I am sending you what my Father promised. As for you, stay in the city [of Jerusalem] until you are empowered from on high" (Luke 24:49). As the opening of Acts recounts, "While he was with them [his disciples], he commanded them not to leave Jerusalem, but to wait for the Father's promise. 'Which,' he said, 'you have heard me speak about; for John baptized with water, but you will be baptized with the Holy Spirit in a few days'" (Acts 1:4–5). Jesus harkened back to the words of John the Baptist: the Messiah would baptize with the Holy Spirit. Amplifying this expectation, Jesus indicated that this fresh, unprecedented outpouring was just around the corner.

The disciples' excitement must have been palpable!

The beginning of the fulfillment of this long-anticipated promise took place soon afterward:

> When the day of Pentecost had arrived, they
> [Jesus's disciples] were all together in one place.
> Suddenly a sound like that of a violent rushing
> wind came from heaven, and it filled the whole
> house where they were staying. They saw tongues
> like flames of fire that separated and rested on
> each one of them. Then they were all filled with
> the Holy Spirit and began to speak in different
> tongues, as the Spirit enabled them. (Acts 2:1–4)

Prophesied by Jeremiah. Projected by Ezekiel. Predicted by
Joel. Proclaimed by John the Baptist. Promised by Jesus Christ.
Poured out on Pentecost. This was the original baptism with the
Spirit. Pulling from Joel's prophecy, Peter confirmed this truth:
"God has raised this Jesus; we are all witnesses of this. Therefore,
since he has been exalted to the right hand of God and has received
from the Father the promised Holy Spirit, he has poured out what
you both see and hear" (Acts 2:32–33).

Baptism with the Spirit is not a mighty work of God confined
to that first Pentecost. On the contrary, it is the work of Jesus
Christ to bless every Christian at the beginning of their salvation.
As John the Baptist underscored, the Messiah would be "the one
who baptizes with the Holy Spirit" (John 1:33). An ongoing ministry of Jesus is His pouring out of the Spirit on His new disciples.
He inundates them with the Holy Spirit!

This point bears repeating. There is a bit of confusion about
who does this work. Some Christians hold that it is the Spirit
who baptizes new believers. But that is wrong or, at the least, not

sufficiently precise.[3] It is Jesus Christ who baptizes new Christians. And for what purpose does Jesus do this? According to Paul, "We were all baptized by [in/with] one Spirit into one body—whether Jews or Greeks, whether slaves or free—and we were all given one Spirit to drink" (1 Cor. 12:13). The purpose of Jesus baptizing His new disciples is to incorporate them into His body, the church.

Upon closer examination of this verse, three points emerge. First, though Paul doesn't state it, Jesus is the one who baptizes. This point about the agent of baptism with the Spirit lines up well with John the Baptist's promise (noted above) that Jesus Christ would baptize with the Spirit. Second, "we all" refers to all Christians, so this mighty act of Jesus takes place as people embrace the gospel and become His disciples.[4] There is no such thing as a non-Spirit baptized Christian. Third, Jesus baptizes His new followers with the Spirit; the Spirit is the element with which they are inundated. The Spirit doesn't baptize new believers with Himself. He doesn't pour Himself out on new disciples of Jesus. The Spirit doesn't give Himself for Christians to drink (that is, taste or experience). No, Jesus does the outpouring, and the element with which (or, better, whom) He inundates His new followers is the Holy Spirit. Jesus is the one who gives the Spirit to imbibe (that is, encounter). Baptism is *with*, not *by*, the Spirit.

A final clarification. Baptism with the Holy Spirit is different from, though related to, two other important experiences of salvation. First, it is different from regeneration. Being born again is the

---

3. For example, the language of the *Baptist Faith and Message* 2000, II C, needs to be more precise.

4. For a strong argument in favor of this point, see John R. W. Stott, *The Baptism and Fullness of the Holy Spirit* (Downers Grove, IL: InterVarsity Press, 1964), 21.

work of the Holy Spirit, and the purpose of this regeneration is the removal of one's old nature and the implanting of a new nature. The agent—the one acting—is the Holy Spirit, and the purpose is a change of nature.

Second, baptism with the Spirit is different from the filling with, or indwelling of, the Spirit. It is the Spirit who fills believers, and the purpose of His indwelling is to render the presence of the triune God, empower for mission, produce Christlikeness, and much more. The agent—the one acting—is the Holy Spirit, and the purpose, briefly, is sanctification.

> Being born again is the work of the Holy Spirit, and the purpose of this regeneration is the removal of one's old nature and the implanting of a new nature. The agent–the one acting–is the Holy Spirit, and the purpose is a change of nature.

Contrast regeneration and indwelling with baptism with the Spirit. In this case, the agent—the one acting—is Jesus Christ. It is Jesus who does the baptizing. And the purpose is to incorporate new believers into the body of Christ, the church. It is not to change their nature, but to unite them into Jesus's church.

		the agent of our experience	the purpose of our experience
our experience	regeneration	the Spirit	transformation of our nature
	filling/indwelling	the Spirit	ongoing sanctification
	baptism with the Spirit	Jesus Christ	incorporation into the church

In summary of these three experiences, at work are different agents. In regeneration, the agent—the one acting—is the Holy Spirit. The same is true with filling/indwelling. The agent—the one acting—is the Holy Spirit. By contrast, in the case of baptism with the Spirit, the agent—the one acting—is Jesus Christ. The purposes are also different. For regeneration, it is transformation of our nature. For filling/indwelling, the purpose is ongoing sanctification. In the case of baptism with the Spirit, the purpose is incorporation into the church. Though related and all involving the Holy Spirit, regeneration, filling/indwelling, and baptism with the Spirit are different divine acts leading to different experiences.

The Debate over Baptism with the Spirit

What I've just presented about the experience of baptism with the Spirit represents the view that's held by one segment of Christianity. As noted in the introduction to this chapter, there are other segments that take a different view of this mighty act of God: Pentecostal churches and the various charismatic movements have a different understanding. How these segments came to be, and what the distinctives of their view are, can be summed up in terms of three developments.[5]

In the first development, toward the beginning of the twentieth century, a group of Christians claimed to have experienced a second blessing some time after their conversion to Jesus Christ. They found many similarities between this second blessing and what happened to the apostles on the day of Pentecost, especially the phenomenon of speaking in tongues. Not surprisingly, then, this group became associated with the name "Pentecostalism."

Three distinct features emerged in Pentecostalism. One distinctive is that some time after a person believes the gospel, converts, and becomes a Christian, she experiences baptism with the Holy Spirit. This powerful work of the Spirit enflames a more intense worship of God, so that she truly loves Him with all her heart. It invigorates her prayer life, which may have been absent or meager. It gives her power to unashamedly share the gospel, replacing fear with courageous witness. Baptism with the Spirit augments her love for others in compassionate, self-sacrificing ways.

A second distinctive is that she speaks in tongues as a confirmation of having received this baptism with the Holy Spirit. She praises God in the very core of her being, but she doesn't understand with her mind what she is praying. This mystery is due to the fact that she speaks to God in a language that she has never spoken nor studied before. Or, if it's not an identifiable language (like Arabic or Swahili), it's some kind of encoded message (for example, X 17 fb 39 Th) that she doesn't understand. Deep within herself, however, she knows that she is speaking praises to the Lord (1 Cor. 14).

---

5. For further discussion, see Allison and Köstenberger, *The Holy Spirit*, 464–70.

A third distinctive is that the Pentecostal church of which she's a part believes that the Spirit continues to give all the spiritual gifts today. These gifts are not only the familiar ones like teaching, leading, administrating, and giving. They include seven other gifts as well: prophecy, word of knowledge, word of wisdom, healings, miracles, speaking in tongues, and interpretation of tongues. These gifts are regularly practiced in her church's worship services. They also contribute powerfully to the personal spirituality of church members.[6]

These three features associated with baptism with the Spirit became the distinctives of Pentecostalism. As a movement, it gave birth to Pentecostal churches and new denominations such as the Assemblies of God and the Church of God (Cleveland, Tennessee). Today, Pentecostalism continues to be a powerful force for the spread of Christianity worldwide.

In the second development, toward the middle of the twentieth century, these Pentecostal features were picked up by mainline denominations such as the Roman Catholic Church, Episcopal churches, Methodist churches, and many more. The distinctives of this Pentecostal influence—especially its emphasis on the gifts of prophecy, speaking in tongues, healings, and so forth—led to it being called the *charismatic movement*, after the biblical word *charismata* for gifts of the Spirit. For example, Paul writes,

- According to the grace given to us, we have different gifts (*charismata*) (Rom. 12:6).
- Now there are different gifts (*charismata*), but the same Spirit (1 Cor. 12:4).

---

6. We will return to this topic of the Spirit's debated gifts in chapter 18.

This word *charismata* became attached to this mid-twentieth-century movement of the Spirit. Like the Pentecostal phenomenon, this charismatic movement expanded exponentially and can be found in many Christian denominations. Because this movement developed out of Pentecostalism, the "first wave" of a new baptism with the Spirit, the charismatic movement is also called the "second wave" of this experience.

Due to the popularity of "first wave" Pentecostalism and "second wave" charismatic movement, a reaction arose among churches and denominations that disagree with the three distinct Pentecostal/charismatic features. These non-Pentecostal and non-charismatic groups (for example, Reformed churches and Bible churches) developed their own three-point counter emphases.[7]

The first counter feature is that baptism with the Holy Spirit takes place at the beginning of salvation and not some time afterward as a second blessing. That is, along with regeneration, union with Christ, justification, and adoption, another one of the mighty acts of God to save people is Jesus's baptism of His new disciples with the Holy Spirit. As an initial experience of salvation, it is not, nor can it be, a subsequent experience sometime after conversion.

The second counter distinctive of these non-Pentecostal and non-charismatic groups is that this experience of baptism with the Spirit is not signaled to have occurred by speaking in tongues. On the contrary, there is no necessary manifestation or apparent validation of being baptized with the Spirit. This absence of speaking in tongues as confirmation of being baptized by the Spirit is due to the last distinctive.

---

7. These counter features were already present in these churches and denominations. Due to the Pentecostal/charismatic phenomena, these three points became counter emphases of these groups.

The third counter feature is that while most spiritual gifts continue today, certain other ones have ceased. That is, the Holy Spirit continues to distribute the familiar gifts like teaching, leading, administrating, and serving to the church today. However, He has ceased to give the seven gifts (listed above): prophecy, word of knowledge, word of wisdom, healings, miracles, speaking in tongues, and interpretation of tongues.[8]

As if the confusion between Pentecostal and charismatic distinctive features and those of non-Pentecostal and non-charismatic distinctive features isn't enough, further commotion arose with the final development in our story.

In the third development, in the early 1980s, some evangelical churches that were identified with neither Pentecostal churches (first wave) nor charismatic movements (second wave) developed another approach, called third wave *evangelicalism*. From the Pentecostal/charismatic distinctives, these churches took the feature of the continuation of all spiritual gifts. From the non-Pentecostal/non-charismatic distinctives, they took baptism with the Spirit as the mighty act of Jesus Christ to pour out the Spirit at the beginning of salvation. These churches did not consider baptism with the Spirit to be a second blessing, an experience some time after conversion. Additionally, third wave proponents rejected speaking in tongues as a necessary sign of having been baptized by the Spirit. That gift may accompany the initial experience of Spirit baptism—after all, it is one of the gifts of the Spirit—but it does not necessarily function as a confirmation of that experience.

First wave Pentecostalism. Second wave charismatic movement. Third wave evangelicalism. These three positions are at the

---

8. Again, the reason for the continuation of certain gifts and the cessation of other gifts will be the topic of chapter 18.

heart of the debate over baptism with the Spirit. Not to be lost in this confusion are the many points that the three views share in common:

- The necessity of the work of the Holy Spirit for initiation into salvation and continued growth in it.
- The Spirit's distribution of spiritual gifts for the maturity and multiplication of the church.
- The experience of baptism with the Spirit— whenever it takes place—for the fullness of blessing and eternal life.

Even in the midst of debate, this topic calls for application.

1. What has been your experience of baptism with the Holy Spirit? Had you heard of it before reading this chapter? Was it something that is sometimes mentioned in your church but not emphasized? Was it a second blessing in your life? Did you speak in tongues when you were baptized with the Spirit?

2. Is the discussion on the differences between baptism with the Spirit, regeneration, and the filling with the Spirit helpful? How and why are these related but diverse experiences important for you?

3. Are you a first wave Pentecostal, a second wave charismatic, a non-Pentecostal/non-charismatic, or a third wave evangelical? Why?

4. Do you think it is possible to develop some kind of consensus among these diverse groups? Why would such agreement—partial as it is—be important to the church of Jesus Christ today?

CHAPTER 9

The Holy Spirit's Work of Salvation (Part 2)

In chapter 7, I presented the Spirit's work at the beginning of salvation. He initiates our rescue from sin through regeneration, conversion, union with Christ, justification, and adoption. What the Spirit begins, He continues and develops throughout our entire lifetime. In this chapter, I focus on the ongoing mighty acts of the Holy Spirit that stretch from the start of our Christian life and continue until either our death or Christ's return. These mighty works are sealing, sanctification, and assurance of salvation.

Sealing

The Holy Spirit seals believers, guaranteeing their salvation.[1] This divine marking—like sealing an envelope shut by dampening

---

1. For further discussion, see Gregg R. Allison and Andreas J. Köstenberger, *The Holy Spirit: Theology for the People of God* (Nashville: B&H Academic, 2020), 395–96.

the glue and folding it over—takes place when people trust the work of Christ through the hearing of the gospel. It is a guarantee that God will keep His children throughout their life so that they will ultimately obtain His promised inheritance: the fullness of salvation as eternal life.

> In him [Christ] you were sealed with the promised Holy Spirit when you heard the word of truth, the gospel of your salvation, and when you believed. The Holy Spirit is the down payment of our inheritance, until the redemption of the possession, to the praise of his glory (Eph. 1:13–14; also 2 Cor. 1:22; 5:5).

The promised Holy Spirit is the seal, or guarantee, of salvation.

Through His works of regeneration, conversion, union with Christ, justification, and adoption, the Holy Spirit has initiated our salvation. Still, that salvation is both partial and promised. That is, we have salvation in part: God's presence in our life—in part. Christ's perfect model of holiness that we follow—in part. The Spirit's powerful work in overcoming temptation and sin—in part. The church's instruction and discipling toward Christlikeness—in part. So, salvation is also promised. That is, one day we will have salvation in full: God's presence in our life—in full, as we will see Him face-to-face. Christ's perfect model of holiness that we follow—in full, as we will be completely conformed to His image. The Spirit's powerful work in overcoming temptation and sin—in full, when we will be

The promised Holy Spirit is the seal, or guarantee, of salvation.

totally released from even the presence of sin. The church's instruction and discipling toward Christlikeness—in full, when the church will be the perfect bride of Christ.

Between this partial salvation and its promised fullness, the Holy Spirit is a seal. As such, He marks out believers as participants in God's mighty work that has begun and that will be completed. Paul uses other images for this sealing:

> He is the divine down payment, a type of earnest money paid with the promise of the remainder still to be remunerated. The Holy Spirit is the firstfuits, the initial portion of the harvest that is gathered in anticipation of the rest still to be reaped. He is the guarantee for believers that "he who started a good work in you will carry it on to completion until the day of Christ Jesus." (Phil. 1:6)[2]

The Holy Spirit as a seal is like a down payment, the firstfruits, the guarantee of salvation.

The sealing of the Spirit leads Christians in two specific ways. First, and in line with Paul's command, they have a strong deterrent to sinning: "Don't grieve God's Holy Spirit. You were sealed by him for the day of redemption" (Eph. 4:30). With their salvation guaranteed, with their inheritance completely secure, why would Christians disobey, mistrust, and/or rebel against God and thus sadden the Holy Spirit whose mark they bear? The Spirit prompts and empowers believers to avoid sinning.

---

2. Allison and Köstenberger, *The Holy Spirit*, 396.

Second, and again in line with Paul's exhortation, Christians long for the completion of salvation: "we ourselves who have the Spirit as the firstfruits—we also groan within ourselves, eagerly waiting for adoption, the redemption of our bodies" (Rom. 8:23).

> The Holy Spirit as our seal—the firstfruits—leads to intense longing for Christ to redeem us fully and forever.

This "groaning" is not the moaning of pain or the sadness of disappointment. Rather, it is the deep, unceasing yearning for Christ to return to bring salvation in its fullness. Then, and only then, will our adoption be completed in the sense that we in our wholeness will belong to God. Then, and only then, will we be resurrected and thus be fully conformed to the image of Christ—bearing His image in our glorified body. The Holy Spirit as our seal—the firstfruits—leads to intense longing for Christ to redeem us fully and forever.

Sanctification

At the start of chapter 2, I asked this question: As you look back over the course of your Christian life, how can you account for the growth that you see? I then proposed that your list probably included some or all of the following items:

- *the Bible:* reading, memorizing, studying, praying, and applying the Word of God
- *prayer:* reciting the Lord's Prayer, praising and thanking God, voicing requests for yourself and for others, and interceding for concerns at your church

- *church:* worship, singing, confessing sin, giving, listening to sermons, and celebrating baptism and the Lord's Supper
- *small group participation:* studying the Bible together with others, fellowshipping with other church members in a community group, engaging in outreach as part of a missional community
- *spiritual disciplines:* fasting, silence, mortifying sin, journaling, and accountability
- *service:* using your spiritual gifts (such as teaching, leading, administrating, and exhorting) at church, evangelizing, discipling new believers, mentoring those in crisis, and supporting missions
- *life events:* suffering, forgiving others, celebrating milestones (such as graduations, marriages, and births), and grieving tragedies (such as dire medical prognoses, onset of Alzheimer's, and deaths)

I also expressed hope that your list includes another important item—the Holy Spirit—that helps account for your growth as a Christian over the course of time. Why is He so important in this way?

One of the Spirit's mighty, ongoing works is sanctification, or progressive growth into Christlikeness.[3] Put differently, sanctifica-

---

3. For further discussion, see Allison and Köstenberger, *The Holy Spirit*, 407–13.

tion is the ongoing transformation from sinfulness to holiness as Christians mature into fully devoted followers of Christ.

Sanctification is a cooperative enterprise: God and believers together contribute to those believers growing more and more into the image of Christ. Paul highlights this collaboration when he urges Christians to "work out your own salvation with fear and trembling. For it is God who is working in you both to will and to work according to his good purpose" (Phil. 2:12–13). On the one hand, Christians work out their salvation. On the other hand, God works out their salvation, providing the will and the effort for them to carry out God's good purpose of sanctification.

> Sanctification is a cooperative enterprise: God and believers together contribute to those believers growing more and more into the image of Christ.

God's work in sanctification includes many elements. Examples include the provision of His inspired Word, protection from the onslaughts of the evil one, and the example of Jesus Christ. Most important for our purposes, the Holy Spirit takes primary place: God provides "the sanctifying work of the Holy Spirit" (1 Pet. 1:2). Specifically, the Spirit convicts of sin, prompts repentance, ignites faith, comforts in desperate situations, rebukes in times of rebellion, empowers in the overcoming of temptation, and develops a willingness and an effort to please God. Prayer for God to sanctify His people is an expression of faith that He indeed will do it. As Paul prays, "Now may the God of peace himself sanctify you completely. And may your whole spirit, soul, and body be kept sound and blameless at the coming

of our Lord Jesus Christ. He who calls you is faithful; he will do it"
(1 Thess. 5:23–24).

Believers' work in sanctification consists of both an active
part and a passive part. Importantly, the Holy Spirit is featured in
both aspects. Christians play their active role by reading the Bible,
praying, putting sin to death, engaging in spiritual disciplines—
the items listed above. All of these activities are done through the
presence and power of the Spirit. Christians play their passive role
by yielding to the Spirit, consciously being filled with/walking by/
keeping in step with/setting their minds on/being guided by the
Spirit.[4]

This "passivity" doesn't mean believers just wait around until
the Spirit prompts them to do something. After all, they are actively
engaged in the sanctification process, so "let God and let go" isn't
an option for them. At the same time, this "activity" doesn't mean
that Christians forge on ahead, making their plans, running their
programs, and engaging in frenetic "work for God" while asking
the Spirit to bless their attempts. Rather, the Spirit is the initiator,
the foundation for the believers' active role in sanctification. They
follow the Spirit, echoing Paul's prayer "that our God will make
[us] worthy of his calling, and by his power fulfill [our] every desire
to do good and [our] work produced by faith" (2 Thess. 1:11).

The situation was a desperate one, yet one in which the Spirit's
prompting was clear in my life. Misunderstanding abounded. Trust
had been broken. Suspicion colored every conversation. Truth was
in short supply. Several people—I included—had sinfully con-
tributed to the mess. Someone proposed a meeting where all sides
could voice their concerns and complaints. That idea morphed into

---

4. These items will be the focus of chapters 14 and 15.

a proposal for a listening session. I was undone and couldn't see clearly what I should do.

A serious conversation ensued with dear friends. Asking their counsel, I wondered what approach I should take. Unexpectedly, one friend offered clearly and firmly, "I think the Holy Spirit wants you just to confess your sins." He quickly followed up, "Don't complain. Don't criticize. Don't explain. Don't try to justify yourself. Just confess your sins." He finished, "And if the others want anything else from you, just assure them that confession is all that the Holy Spirit wants you to do."

There are some moments in life that are weightier than others. This was one of those times for me. A Holy Spirit moment, we sensed. Surprisingly, it had to do with confession of sin. Not with how to listen well. Not with how to explain myself. Not with how to resolve the entrenched problem overall. Just confession of sin. But upon further reflection, it wasn't so strange or unexpected, because the *Spirit of holiness* prompts us to acknowledge our sins, admit we are wrong, and repent of them. And when those sins are against other people, the Holy Spirit prompts us to confess them to others.

Following the Spirit's prompting to confess my sins, I confessed my sins. Period. It was a Holy Spirit moment prompting toward sanctification, holiness of life.

So, sanctification is not moralism, behaviorism, and legalism. Moralism directs believers to keep God's law in an attempt to merit salvation from Him. Behaviorism instructs Christians to act Christlike without being concerned with loving and pleasing God from their heart. Legalism constructs additional rules to obey and sins to avoid, adding to the Bible in a self-righteous attempt to appear holy in ways beyond what God reveals in His Word. These three false approaches to sanctification do not have God's blessing and ultimately do not contribute to believers breaking from sin and becoming more Christlike.

Rather, sanctification is a progressive transformation that entails, with regard to sin, a deeper realization of it, distaste for it, confession of it, repentance from it, and killing of it. This repudiation and overcoming of sin is never a merely human effort but is always empowered by the Holy Spirit.

Scripture denounces sin, which is linked to opposition to the Spirit. After all, He is the *Holy* Spirit who calls us to fight against and surmount sin and thus become more holy. As Paul urges us, "Don't grieve God's Holy Spirit. You were sealed by him for the day of redemption" (Eph. 4:30). Why would we ever act to sadden the Spirit, the seal of our salvation, by our sin? Similarly, Paul exhorts us, "Don't stifle the Spirit" (1 Thess. 5:19). This command imagines us throwing water on a fire so as to put it out. The descent of the Holy Spirit on Pentecost is linked with fire (Acts 2:3), indicative of His powerful work. Why would we ever douse the activity of the Spirit who empowers us to walk in God's way? We must avoid sinning against the Holy Spirit. Put positively, "through the Spirit's enabling presence, believers curb their appetites, contain their desires, curtail their actions, check their words. Indeed, self-control is a fruit of the Spirit (Gal. 5:22–23)."[5]

There is one particular sin against the Holy Spirit that causes much debate and consternation among Christians.[6] Blasphemy against the Holy Spirit is the unpardonable sin. Jesus addresses it in His rebuke of the religious leaders of His day:

---

5. Allison and Köstenberger, *The Holy Spirit*, 411.
6. This section is adapted from Allison and Köstenberger, *The Holy Spirit*, 343–45.

Then a demon-possessed man who was blind and unable to speak was brought to him. He healed him, so that the man could both speak and see. All the crowds were astounded and said, "Could this be the Son of David?"

When the Pharisees heard this, they said, "This man drives out demons only by Beelzebul, the ruler of the demons."

Knowing their thoughts, he told them, "Every kingdom divided against itself is headed for destruction, and no city or house divided against itself will stand. If Satan drives out Satan, he is divided against himself. How then will his kingdom stand? And if I drive out demons by Beelzebul, by whom do your sons drive them out? For this reason they will be your judges. If I drive out demons by the Spirit of God, then the kingdom of God has come upon you. How can someone enter a strong man's house and steal his possessions unless he first ties up the strong man? Then he can plunder his house. Anyone who is not with me is against me, and anyone who does not gather with me scatters. Therefore, I tell you, people will be forgiven every sin and blasphemy, but the blasphemy against the Spirit will not be forgiven. Whoever speaks a word against the Son of Man, it will be forgiven him; but whoever speaks against the Holy Spirit, it will not be forgiven him, either in this age or in the one to come." (Matt. 12:22–32)

Jesus denounces blasphemy against the Holy Spirit.

Four interpretations of this unpardonable sin are offered.[7] The first understanding is that blasphemy is evil, absurd dismissal and insulting of the Spirit. Though the Spirit bears witness to Jesus Christ, those who blaspheme the Spirit ascribe that work to Satan instead. Support for this view closely follows Matthew's Gospel (cited above). Jesus performed a miracle by the Holy Spirit. His opponents hatefully and unreasonably claimed that the miracle was actually empowered by Satan. They denounced the testimony of the Spirit to Christ, smearing the Spirit's work and ascribing it to the evil one. They committed blasphemy against the Holy Spirit.

The second interpretation, modifying the first, is that while this sin could be committed in Jesus's day, no one can blaspheme the Spirit today. This view is based on the fact that Jesus is no longer casting out demons by the Holy Spirit. Thus, blasphemy against the Spirit is not possible. It could only be committed during Jesus's earthly ministry.

The third understanding moves beyond this episode in Jesus's ministry to consider other biblical teachings about sin. It considers blasphemy against the Holy Spirit to be unbelief in Christ throughout a person's entire life. This refusal to believe the gospel for salvation endures till the very end. This persistent unbelief signifies that the person cannot be forgiven.

The fourth interpretation, also broadening beyond this narrative of Jesus exorcising a demon, is apostasy. By this sin, a person who once was a Christian abandons their faith in Jesus and thus loses their salvation. This view appeals to the warning in Hebrews

---

7. For further discussion, see Herman Bavinck, *Reformed Dogmatics*, vol. 3: *Sin and Salvation in Christ*, ed. John Bolt, trans. John Vriend (Grand Rapids: Baker Academic, 2006), 155–57.

about the danger of falling away: "it is impossible to renew to repentance" Christians who have committed apostasy (Heb. 6:4) because "they are recrucifying the Son of God and holding him up to contempt" (v. 6). They have blasphemed against the Holy Spirit and their sin is unforgiveable.

These four positions have solid biblical support and, despite their differences, agree on the most important point of all: blasphemy against the Holy Spirit is the most serious sin and is unpardonable. But why is it unforgiveable? It is not as though Christ did not die for that particular sin, because He died for all sins, even the most heinous. Rather, this sin can't be forgiven because the one who commits it has a heart so callous, so cold, so closed to the work of the Holy Spirit that they cannot embrace the gospel. Having rejected the one who convicts of sin, regenerates, unites with Christ, prompts faith for justification, and more, those who blaspheme the Spirit have no hope of salvation.

Interestingly, one of the most common questions I get as a theologian has to do with this sin. I'm asked, "Do you think I've committed blasphemy against the Holy Spirit?" Once a pastor told an elderly woman that she had committed this sin when she had a particularly bad dream. She asked me if I thought it was true. A man confessed he had been deeply involved in occult practices as a teenager, so he was fearful he had blasphemed against the Spirit. He wondered if I agreed. My response usually points to the worry and fear that grips these people. These are signs of sensitivity to the Spirit. They are certainly not indications of dismissing, insulting, denouncing, and smearing the Spirit, ascribing His work instead to Satan. "No," I respond to these questioners, "you've not committed blasphemy against the Holy Spirit."

The third concrete way that sanctification shows itself in the lives of Christians has to do with holiness or Christlikeness. As they mature, believers exhibit a deepening passion for becoming Christlike. They pursue holiness more fervently. They regularly consecrate themselves to godliness.

Specifically, sanctification delights in the two greatest commandments as set forth by Jesus: "Love the Lord your God with all your heart, with all your soul, and with all your mind. This is the greatest and most important command. The second is like it: Love your neighbor as yourself. All the Law and the Prophets depend on these two commands" (Matt. 22:37–40). Those who are being sanctified embrace the blessings of Jesus's beatitudes, seek conformity to God's commands from the heart, love their enemies, and give secretly. They pray as Jesus taught, treasure God above all else, refuse to worry, and don't judge. Those pursuing sanctification live the "golden rule" ("whatever you want others to do for you, do also the same for them" [Matt. 7:12]), welcome the kingdom, and build on the rock (Matt. 5–7).

Ultimately, sanctification refuses to see the above virtues as achievable by human effort alone, or even by human effort plus a little help from God. Rather, genuine progressive transformation into the image of Jesus Christ depends on the presence and power of the Spirit.

Assurance

Because of the sealing of the Holy Spirit and His work of sanctification, Christians may enjoy the subjective confidence that they belong to God forever and will remain Christians throughout their entire lifetime.[8] Such subjective confidence is the assurance of salvation. This persuasion is not self-generated, mustered up because of some high level of trust in God. It's not due to an impressive amount of obedience to Him and/or fruitfulness in ministry. This assurance is not the privilege of a select few, the elite super-spiritual members of the church. On the contrary, this confidence may belong to each and every person who genuinely trusts in Christ for salvation.

Sadly, many Christians lack the assurance of salvation. This absence may be due to a lack of teaching about assurance. It may be due to poor teaching about—even the denial of—assurance. As some church leaders reason, if Christians are confident they will be saved, they might lose the motivation to live for Christ. They might become lax in their sanctification and drift away from the faith, even to the point of losing their salvation. The result of such thinking is that these church leaders don't affirm and teach assurance of salvation, keeping Christians in doubt about their promised end. Additionally, the lack of assurance may be caused by depression (which is often accompanied by hopelessness), persistent sin (which rightly disturbs them of their salvation), and even attacks by Satan and demons. One of the greatest strategies of the evil one is to disturb Christians about their salvation, thereby paralyzing them with fear and worry.

But assurance of salvation, when properly grounded and understood, is a welcomed benefit and abiding comfort for all Christians. First, assurance is linked to perseverance. This is the mighty act of God to preserve true Christians by His power through their faith for the salvation that is ready for them to inherit in its fulness

---

8. For further discussion, see Allison and Köstenberger, *The Holy Spirit*, 396–98.

(1 Pet. 1:5). Perseverance is a divine work; God holds genuine believers in Christ. He does so through the instruction of His Word, sanctification by the Spirit, empowerment to face down and overcome temptation, participation in church worship services, spiritual disciplines, protection from Satan, and the very presence of God Himself. Because of this divine work of perseverance, Christians may enjoy the assurance of salvation. They may know that nothing can ever separate them "from the love of God that is in Christ Jesus our Lord" (Rom. 8:39).

> Perseverance is a divine work; God holds genuine believers in Christ.

Second, assurance of salvation is a work of the Holy Spirit, as noted earlier:

> You did not receive a spirit of slavery to fall back into fear. Instead, you received the Spirit of adoption, by whom we cry out, "*Abba*, Father!" The Spirit himself testifies together with our spirit that we are God's children, and if children, also heirs— heirs of God and coheirs with Christ—if indeed we suffer with him so that we may also be glorified with him. (Rom. 8:15–17)

The Holy Spirit of adoption casts out enslaving fear. Christians never have to fear sin overcoming them and/or the evil one overpowering them. The Spirit of adoption enables Jesus's disciples to vocally acknowledge the Fatherhood of God, who loves them with a love that will not fail or expire. The Spirit provides assurance of salvation, His "inner witness" or "secret testimony" of the Spirit. He bears witness or testifies to the spirit, or inner core, of Christians. They have a deeply rooted, subjective confidence of adoption, a certainty that they are presently and will always continue to be the beloved children of God. As heirs, they will surely inherit the fullness of salvation, being glorified through being fully conformed to the image of Christ.

I still vividly recall the first thought that flooded my mind when I called out to God to save me—"Now you have eternal life." It was not as though Zeke, as he shared his testimony, mentioned eternal life. It was not due to a pastor teaching about assurance of salvation. Rather, as I learned awhile later by reading the Bible, that promise was the work of the Holy Spirit, granting me the assurance of salvation.

I don't know what the inner witness of the Spirit was/is for you. Some have described it as a confidence of having passed from death to life. Others have described it as a sense of the removal of the awful weight of sin. Still others have described it as finally coming to know the true God after a long search for Him. No matter what form it may take, the manifestation of the Spirit of adoption is the privilege of all who embrace Jesus Christ as Savior and Lord.

Such assurance is not at all for people who just profess faith in Christ.[9] On the contrary, it is only for genuine believers who live as Christ lived: "The one who says he remains in him should walk just as he walked" (1 John 2:6). Perhaps you, as I, know people who go to church and claim to be Christians, but they do not live for Christ. Yes, they have walked the aisle to respond to an altar call. Yes, they have been baptized, either as an infant or after making a profession of faith in Christ. Yes, they have affixed their signature to

---

9. If you are a genuine Christian with a sensitive conscience and start to feel unsure of your salvation, this paragraph is not about you and not for you to apply.

a church membership roll. Tragically, these people have not experienced the reality of salvation. Still, they consider themselves genuine Christians and claim unshakably the assurance of salvation. This notion is not in line with the biblical picture of true Christ-followers and the (rightful) subjective confidence they enjoy.

God grants the assurance of salvation to those who genuinely know and love Him, follow the example of His Son, and walk in the joy and comfort of the Holy Spirit.

There's much to apply from this chapter!

1. How does the sealing work of the Holy Spirit give you hope that the salvation you enjoy in part now will one day give way to salvation in full? Do you think anything—overwhelming temptation, demonic attack, persecution—or anyone—including yourself—can ever separate you from the love of God in Christ? How does the guarantee of the Spirit work to correct your wrong thinking?

2. How would you assess your progress in sanctification? Have there been particular periods in your life in which you made more and steadier progress than in others? What could account for that greater growth? When you've sensed times of dryness and dullness, what could account for that darkness? What steps could you take now to avoid repetition?

To help your assessment, are you particularly pleased or disappointed with any of the following elements (from our earlier list) that contribute to your sanctification?

- the Bible
- prayer
- church

- small group participation
- spiritual disciplines
- life events

In which of these areas do you sense the Spirit wants you to make progress? How can you concretely do so?

3. Do you have the assurance of your salvation? Why or why not? If you have, how would you describe this certainty? How does this assurance encourage you, motivate you, and comfort you?

4. If you lack this assurance, how can this chapter help you gain it? Perhaps you lack assurance because it seems mysterious or even confusing. Hear these straightforward words from John: "This is how we know that we remain in him and he in us: He has given us of his Spirit" (1 John 4:13). This is God's promise to you: He has given the Spirit of adoption to you, His child. Will you trust that promise and thereby know that you belong to Him now and always?

CHAPTER 10

The Holy Spirit's Work of Illumination and Intercession

G od is kind to His people, and this kindness shows up concretely in two ongoing works of the Holy Spirit: His illumination of Scripture and His intercession for Christians.

Illumination

Not only did the Holy Spirit inspire the Bible, He also illumines it.[1] That is, He superintended the biblical authors as they wrote the Bible such that it is God-breathed, true (inerrant), authoritative, sufficient, necessary, clear, and life-transforming. In addition, the

---

1. For further discussion, see Gregg R. Allison and Andreas J. Köstenberger, *The Holy Spirit: Theology for the People of God* (Nashville: B&H Academic, 2020), 317–18.

Spirit illumines inspired Scripture, helping believers understand and apply the Word of God.

As the word *illumination* itself implies, this work of the Spirit has to do with enlightening the eyes and hearts of its readers. Such illumination is necessary, first of all, for unbelievers to understand and embrace the gospel. As Paul explains their hopeless situation:

> But if our gospel is veiled, it is veiled to those who are perishing. In their case, the god of this age has blinded the minds of the unbelievers to keep them from seeing the light of the gospel of the glory of Christ, who is the image of God. For we are not proclaiming ourselves but Jesus Christ as Lord, and ourselves as your servants for Jesus's sake. For God who said, "Let light shine out of darkness," has shone in our hearts to give the light of the knowledge of God's glory in the face of Jesus Christ. (2 Cor. 4:3–6)

Unbelievers find themselves in a dreadful situation. They are blinded by Satan, the god of this world, so that they cannot grasp the light of the gospel. The Spirit's illumination is necessary to open their eyes so that they can believe in Jesus Christ as Lord.

At creation, God spoke the command, "Let there be light!" to overcome the darkness of the original state of the world. For His work of re-creation—salvation through the gospel—God again commands, "Let there be light!" to overcome the debilitating darkness of unbelievers in their state of fallenness—blindness due to Satan. The Spirit's work of illumination is designed to remove their blindness so that they may see and embrace the gospel. As Martin Luther reminds us, "The truth is that nobody who has not the

Spirit of God sees a jot [bit] of what is in the Scriptures. . . . The Spirit is needed for the understanding of all Scripture and every part of Scripture."[2]

As Luther notes, this illuminating ministry of the Spirit continues for believers to enable them to understand all of Scripture. Whereas the Bible itself is clear, even believers still beset by sin need light to shine to overcome the darkness of their misunderstanding of it. Such lack of comprehension may be due to various factors: Not reading biblical passages in their context. Approaching Scripture with the wrong expectations. Trying to defend a mistaken theological position. Attempting to show off the superiority of one's biblical knowledge. Lacking the necessary attitudes and virtues (for example, humility and peacefulness) for proper understanding. The illumination of Scripture overcomes these weaknesses and errors. At the same time, this work is not a substitute for careful study and understanding of the Bible, following well-proven principles of interpretation. Pay attention to the meaning of words and sentences. Read passages in their biblical and historical context. Seek to know Christ.

God is kind to His people, and this kindness shows up concretely in two ongoing works of the Holy Spirit: His illumination of Scripture and His intercession for Christians.

---

2. Martin Luther, *The Bondage of the Will*, trans. James I. Packer and O. R. Johnston (Old Tappan, NJ: Revell, 1957), 73–74. *Luther's Works* 33:28.

Scripture underscores the Spirit's work of illumination, which is second in a chain of two events. First, God inspired the writing of His Word. As Peter notes, this superintending of the biblical authors has special reference to the Holy Spirit, who moved them as "they spoke [= wrote] from God" (2 Pet. 1:21). In Paul's words, the apostles, under the inspiration of the Spirit, spoke (= wrote) biblical truth, "not in words taught by human wisdom, but in those taught by the Spirit" (1 Cor. 2:13).

Second, God illumines the reading/hearing of His Word. This reading/hearing engages two types of recipients. The first group consists of unbelievers: "The natural person does not accept the things of the Spirit of God, for they are folly to him, and he is not able to understand them because they are spiritually discerned" (2:14 ESV). Unbelievers, when they read/hear the Bible, lack the Spirit and His ministry of illumination. Thus, they do not—indeed, cannot—understand the Bible. The second group consists of believers: "The spiritual person judges all things, but is himself to be judged by no one. 'For who has understood the mind of the Lord so as to instruct him?' But we have the mind of Christ" (2:15–16 ESV). Believers enjoy the privilege of having the Spirit and His work of illumination. Thus, they can understand Scripture. Through constant exposure to and proper understanding of the Word of God, believers develop "the mind of Christ."

This work of the Holy Spirit does not just engage with understanding Scripture. Beyond helping believers to grasp the meaning of Scripture, the Spirit softens their hearts so that they are ready to apply Scripture properly. Listen to this prayer for the Spirit's illumination:

> Almighty, eternal, and merciful God, whose
> Word is a lamp unto our feet and a light unto

our path, open and illuminate our minds, that we may purely and perfectly understand your Word and that our lives may be conformed to what we have rightly understood, that in nothing we may be displeasing unto your majesty, through Jesus Christ our Lord. Amen.[3]

This prayer for illumination could/should become a regular practice before believers open their Bibles. In prayer, they ask the Spirit to help them rightly understand the meaning of Scripture and properly apply that meaning in concrete ways. These applications may take the form of praise offered to God, thanksgiving for His grace and provision, trust in His promises, obedience to His commands, confession of sin—whatever Scripture calls for in terms of proper application of its rightly understood instructions.

Intercession

A second ongoing work of the Holy Spirit is His intercession on behalf of believers.[4] When they don't know how or what to pray, the Spirit prays. Paul's instruction about this work is both honest and hopeful:

In the same way the Spirit also helps us in our weakness, because we do not know what to pray for as we should, but the Spirit himself intercedes for us with inexpressible groanings. And he who

---

3. Gottfried W. Locher, *Zwingli's Thought: New Perspectives* (Leiden: Brill, 1981), 28.
4. For further discussion, see Allison and Köstenberger, *The Holy Spirit*, 407–8.

searches our hearts knows the mind of the Spirit, because he intercedes for the saints according to the will of God. (Rom. 8:26–27)

Paul underscores the groanings of creation: its "labor pains" are due to its fallen condition and yearning for its freedom "from the bondage of decay" (vv. 21–22). He links these groanings of creation with the groanings of Christians: "we ourselves who have the Spirit as the firstfruits—we also groan within ourselves, eagerly awaiting adoption, the redemption of our bodies" (v. 23).

Paul is honest: Christians struggle to pray because they live as still sinful believers in a sinful world. Especially as they have their backs against the wall—they face trials, temptations, loss, persecution, and other afflictions—they don't know how to pray or don't know what to pray. As they try to hold back the tears of despair, they can't even mouth the words of a prayer to God. Paul's description of our desperate reality is honest.

Paul is also full of hope that, in these times, the Holy Spirit prays on their behalf. He intercedes for distraught Christians, not using human words—English, Korean, Spanish, Italian—but addresses himself to God "with unspoken groanings." This is a divine communication that humans cannot—nor need to—understand. The Spirit appeals on their behalf that the Father will grant comfort, direction, encouragement, hope, relief—whatever is needed in the moment. And the assurance is that the Father, who eternally loves and listens to the Spirit, grants the Spirit's request. Christians have that for which the Spirit prays.

Time for some application.

1. Do you make it a regular practice to pray to the Holy Spirit before you read, meditate on, and study the Bible? If so, what

does that prayer for illumination look like? If not, how can you incorporate that act of dependence prior to trying to understand Scripture?

2. Does your church's liturgy or schedule of elements in its worship service include a time before the reading and preaching of Scripture to ask for the Holy Spirit's illumination of His inspired Word? How might this aspect become part of your church's worship?

3. When you're confused, undone, disoriented, and can't even voice a meager prayer for help, do you take comfort in the intercessory work of the Holy Spirit? Rather than worrying, becoming fearful that you are failing God through your silence, how does Paul's encouragement give you hope that you will have what you require in your moment of need?

CHAPTER 11

The Holy Spirit's Work in the Church

W hile much of the preceding discussion has to do with us individually as Christians affected by the work of the Holy Spirit,
this chapter discusses the Spirit's work in the church.[1] We've already
briefly touched on the church and the Spirit, and later we will
discuss how being filled with the Spirit produces virtues that are
expressed in the church. Now, however, we focus on this corporate
aspect.

Interestingly, when I ask people to define the church, they
often use the image of a body: the church is the body of Christ. Of
course, this definition is true because it is biblical. Speaking of the

---

1. For further discussion, see Gregg R. Allison and Andreas J. Köstenberger,
The Holy Spirit: Theology for the People of God (Nashville: B&H Academic,
2020), 415–55. For an extensive treatment of the doctrine of the church,
see Gregg R. Allison, *Sojourners and Strangers: The Doctrine of the Church*,
Foundations of Evangelical Theology (Wheaton, IL: Crossway, 2012). For
a shorter discussion, see Gregg R. Allison, *The Church: An Introduction*
(Wheaton, IL: Crossway, 2021).

Father's exaltation of the Son, Paul explains: "he [the Father] sub-jected everything under his [the Son's] feet and appointed him as head over everything for the church, which is his body, the fullness of the one who fills all things in every way" (Eph. 1:22–23). Paul extends the image: "Just as the body is one and has many parts, and all the parts of that body, though many, are one body—so also is Christ. . . . Now you are the body of Christ, and individual mem-bers of it" (1 Cor. 12:12, 27).

Despite the popularity of this body image, there is another important yet often overlooked image: the church is the temple of the Holy Spirit. Paul highlights this idea when talking about Christ: "In him the whole building, being put together, grows into a holy temple in the Lord. In him you are also being built together for God's dwelling in the Spirit" (Eph. 2:21–22). As a whole build-ing, the church is a holy temple in which God dwells by the Holy Spirit. To be even clearer, we note Paul's challenge to the church of Corinth: "Don't you yourselves know that you are God's temple and that the Spirit of God lives in you? If anyone destroys God's temple, God will destroy him; for God's temple is holy, and that is what you are" (1 Cor. 3:16–17).

Why do we favor the image of a body and rarely use the image of temple when defining the church? Perhaps it is due to the fact that all of us have a body. Thus, the image is right at hand and easy to understand. As for the image of a temple, when was the last time you went to one? Have you ever even visited a temple? Probably not. With the image so foreign to us, the definition of the church as the temple of the Holy Spirit is easily skipped.

The church, however, is the people of God constituted by both Jesus Christ and the Holy Spirit. Both together established the church. In chapter 4, we explained the two eternal processions of the Trinity and the two temporal missions that flow from those processions. Procession 1 is the eternal generation of the Son from the Father. Procession 2 is the eternal procession of the Holy Spirit from the Father and the Son. Procession 1 expresses itself in the mission of the Son, who became incarnate and accomplished the work of salvation. Procession 2 expresses itself in the mission of the Holy Spirit, who was poured out, indwells, and applies the work of salvation to fallen people. From both missions flows the church as both the body of Christ (procession and mission 1) and the temple of the Holy Spirit (procession and mission 2).

This definition means that while our church should never cease to be Christ-centered and growing in that direction, that orientation is not enough. Our church should also be Spirit-activated, that is, guided, empowered, gifted, transformed, matured, and expanded by the Holy Spirit. Four biblical instructions about the church as Spirit-activated help it to live and engage in ministry as the temple of the Spirit.

First, the Holy Spirit grants unity to the church. As Paul exhorts the church, "make every effort to keep the unity of the Spirit through the bond of peace" (Eph. 4:3). Paul's instruction is not an insistence to work hard to *create* church unity. It is instead an imperative to *maintain* the unity already established by the Spirit. That is, the default mode of the church is harmony. Sadly, through their sin—political maneuvering, infighting, pressing individual agendas, pride, and more—church members wreck that already established harmony. As a consequence, Paul urges the church to expend blood, sweat, and tears to keep the unity of the Spirit.

This unity is fostered by seven commonalities listed by Paul:

> There is one body and one Spirit—just as you
> were called to one hope at your calling—one

Lord, one faith, one baptism, one God and Father
of all, who is above all and through all and in all.
(Eph. 4:4–6)

There are not many churches, but one church. There are not many
spirits, but one Holy Spirit. There is one hope of calling to eternal
life. There is one Jesus Christ who is Lord of all. There is one
faith—"the faith that was delivered to the saints once for all" (Jude
3)—that all Christians believe. There is one sacrament or ordinance
of water baptism, which all Christians have undergone. And there
is one sovereign God who is the
Father of all people in terms of
creating them in His image.

> There are not many churches, but one church. There are not many spirits, but one Holy Spirit. There is one hope of calling to eternal life. There is one Jesus Christ who is Lord of all.

Additionally, four virtues—
"humility and gentleness, with
patience, bearing with one
another in love" (Eph. 4:2)—
help maintain church unity. In a
church characterized by oneness,
its members think more highly
of others than they do of themselves. They are meek rather than
contentious. They steadfastly
work through difficulties. They
put up with one another's idiosyncrasies.

Granted by the Holy Spirit, fostered by seven commonalities,
and aided by four virtues, the unity of the church needs to be main-
tained by its members.

Second, the Spirit establishes leaders in the church. As Paul
preached to the elders of Ephesus, "I did not avoid declaring to
you the whole plan of God. Be on guard for yourselves and for

all the flock of which the Holy Spirit has appointed you as over-seers, to shepherd the church of God, which he purchased with his own blood" (Acts 20:27–28). Elders or pastors[2] are responsible for teaching and preaching, leading the church, praying for its members (especially for the sick), and shepherding God's people. To be qualified for these pastoral responsibilities and empowered to carry them out, these leaders must be established by the Holy Spirit. He equips them, gives them the necessary gifts, matures them, and molds them in proven ministry. As He so works, the Spirit also prompts the church to publicly acknowledge these leaders as its pastors.

Third, the Holy Spirit empowers the church to engage unbelievers with the gospel. Prior to His ascension and the descent of the Spirit, Jesus promised His disciples, "You will receive power when the Holy Spirit has come on you, and you will be my witnesses in Jerusalem, in all Judea and Samaria, and to the ends of the earth" (Acts 1:8). The church is missional as it shares the good news with non-Christians, plants churches, supports and sends missionaries globally, aids the poor and disenfranchised in its community, and more. These missional endeavors are directed and empowered by the Holy Spirit. And He brings about the resulting fruit.

Fourth, the Spirit gives spiritual gifts to the members of the church. Paul explains that "a manifestation of the Spirit is given to each person for the common good. [He then lists a number of gifts.] . . . One and the same Spirit is active in all these, distributing to each person as he wills" (1 Cor. 12:7, 11). That is, each and every church member has a gift or gifts that are given and empowered by

---

2. The terms *pastors* and *elders* are used interchangeably in the New Testament.

the Holy Spirit. As chapter 17 is dedicated to this topic of spiritual gifts, we will pick up the discussion then.

Some application questions for your church:

1. When you focus on the image of the church as the temple of the Holy Spirit, how does/should that image influence how your church lives and engages in ministry?

2. When your members gather together to worship the Lord, do they grow in awareness that the church is the temple of the Holy Spirit? Why or why not? If yes, what particular elements of the worship service help to develop this awareness. If no, what changes could your church make to rectify this problem?

3. Would you say that your church is Spirit-activated, that is, guided, empowered, gifted, transformed, matured, and expanded by the Holy Spirit? If yes, why is it? If no, are there particular areas of your church's life and ministry that you could assist in bringing change?

4. Assess your church as to its unity in the Spirit, its leaders appointed by the Spirit, and its missional engagement empowered by the Spirit. How is your church doing in these three areas? Are there ways you could help to develop these areas?

CHAPTER 12

The Holy Spirit's Work of Perfection

So far, our attention has been directed toward the Spirit's work in the here and now. Of course, His work is not limited to the present but extends into the future.[1] After all, He is described as the seal, the firstfruit, the deposit, and the guarantee. These terms have to do with the future, specifically in regard to salvation. So, the Spirit is future oriented. Even more, the Holy Spirit is directing everything toward its future perfection. This consummation— "bring everything together in Christ, both things in heaven and things on earth" (Eph. 1:10) "so that God may be all in all" (1 Cor. 15:28)—is one of the works of the Spirit.

On the day of Pentecost, the Holy Spirit was poured out. Peter preached about this momentous event, linking it with a prophecy of Joel:

---

1. For further discussion, see Gregg R. Allison and Andreas J. Köstenberger, *The Holy Spirit: Theology for the People of God* (Nashville: B&H Academic, 2020), 457–61.

"And it will be in the last days, says God,
that I will pour out my Spirit on all people;
then your sons and your daughters will prophesy,
your young men will see visions,
and your old men will dream dreams.
I will even pour out my Spirit
on my servants in those days, both men and
women,
and they will prophesy." (Acts 2:17–18)

This prophecy, which began to be inaugurated on Pentecost, describes the present work of the Spirit. In fact, the phrase "in the last days" refers to the entire time between the first and second comings of Jesus Christ. We are "in the last days" and thus we are experiencing the present working of the Holy Spirit.

Interestingly, Peter does not conclude his citation of Joel where we left off. The prophecy continues:

"I will display wonders in the heaven above
and signs on the earth below:
blood and fire and a cloud of smoke.
The sun will be turned to darkness
and the moon to blood
before the great and glorious day of the Lord
comes.
Then everyone who calls
on the name of the Lord will be saved."
(Acts 2:19–21; citing Joel 2:28–32)

Following Joel, Peter announces both the outpouring of the Holy Spirit and the forthcoming "great and glorious day of the Lord." This future event will feature several decisive events: the triumphant return of Jesus Christ, the universal judgment of all humanity, their bodily resurrection, the eternal condemnation of unbelievers, the eternal salvation of believers, and, ultimately, the establishment of the new heaven and new earth.[2] This mighty day of the Lord dawned with the Spirit's outpouring. That event inaugurated the new covenant, gave birth to the church, launched the kingdom of King Jesus, and initiated the age of the Spirit. All these elements operate presently and are ongoing. And all are heading toward their conclusion when Christ will return. To be emphasized is the fact that the Holy Spirit, as the perfector of all the works of God, is working to bring about that grand ending.

> We are "in the last days" and thus we are experiencing the present working of the Holy Spirit.

This day of the Lord has both personal and cosmic aspects tied to the Holy Spirit. As for the personal aspect, when Christ returns and believers experience glorification, the resurrection of their bodies will be the work of the Spirit. As Paul explains, "if the Spirit of him [God the Father] who raised Jesus from the dead lives in you, then he who raised Christ from the dead [God the Father] will also bring your mortal bodies to life through his Spirit who lives in you" (Rom. 8:11). God the Father raised God the Son incarnate through God the Holy Spirit.

As it was for the Son, so it will be for us; our bodily resurrection will be similar to Christ's bodily resurrection—by the Holy Spirit. Then, and only then, will our salvation be complete. Then, and only then, will we be fully conformed to the image of Christ. For

---

2. Some Christians add the millennium to this list.

those who have died before Christ's return and lived as disembodied believers in heaven, then, and only then, will they once again be
full human beings, re-embodied rather than disembodied.[3]

In terms of the cosmic aspect, all creation will be powerfully
transformed. The old universe, fallen as it is, will cease to be. The new
heaven and new earth will mirror the Spirit's original work of creation,
but perfectly redeemed, renewed, and restored. This revitalization—lit-
erally, new life—will involve a purging/destruction of the old creation:[4]

> The heavens will pass away with a loud noise, the
> elements will burn and be dissolved, and the earth
> and the works on it will be disclosed [or "burned
> up"]. Since all these things are to be dissolved in
> this way, it is clear what sort of people you should
> be in holy conduct and godliness as you wait for
> the day of God and hasten its coming. Because of
> that day, the heavens will be dissolved with fire and
> the elements will melt with heat. But based on his
> promise, we wait for new heavens and a new earth,
> where righteousness dwells. (2 Pet. 3:10–13)

The former, sinful, temporary existence will give way to a transformed, perfected, eternal existence.

---

3. For further discussion of the fact that the proper state of human existence is embodiment (whether as embodied people in this earthly life or re-
embodied people following the resurrection), see Gregg R. Allison, *Embodied:
Living as Whole People in a Fractured World* (Grand Rapids: Baker, 2021).

4. Historically, the church has believed that either (1) this event will be a
cleansing of the existing universe and its rejuvenation or (2) this event will
be a destruction of this existing universe and its replacement. In either case,
the church has always affirmed the establishment of the new heaven and new
earth.

Here is the vision of this future reality:

> Then I saw a new heaven and a new earth; for the
> first heaven and the first earth had passed away,
> and the sea was no more. I also saw the holy city,
> the new Jerusalem, coming down out of heaven
> from God, prepared like a bride adorned for her
> husband. Then I heard a loud voice from the throne:
> Look, God's dwelling is with humanity, and he
> will live with them. They will be his peoples, and
> God himself will be with them and will be their
> God. He will wipe away every tear from their eyes.
> Death will be no more; grief, crying, and pain will
> be no more, because the previous things have
> passed away.
>
> Then the one seated on the throne said, "Look,
> I am making everything new." (Rev. 21:1–5)

As it was in the beginning, so it will be in the end. The new, upright, sin-free universe will replace the old, fallen, sin-stained universe. As enabled by the indwelling Spirit, who presently renders the presence of the triune God in believers, so God will dwell with redeemed humanity forever.

Until then, the church relies on the many-sided work of the Holy Spirit and longs for the return of Jesus Christ. As Scripture concludes, "Both the Spirit and the bride say, 'Come!'" (Rev. 22:17).

This future destiny invites some application.

1. Do you regularly think about and long for Christ's return? If so, what difference does it make in your life? If not, why not?

How might regular consideration of this momentous event strengthen your present hope?

2. How does Christ's bodily resurrection encourage you presently if you suffer bodily weaknesses, disabilities, a protracted sickness, even a terminal illness?

3. Do you think it's possible that the experience of the early Christians—who "received the word in much affliction, with the joy of the Holy Spirit" (1 Thess. 1:6 ESV)—can be your experience as well? How could it be?

4. When Peter describes the destruction of the old existence and its replacement with the new heaven and new earth, he makes this application: "it is clear what sort of people you should be in holy conduct and godliness as you wait for the day of God" (2 Pet. 3:11–12). Concretely, what kind of person should you be in light of this future destiny?

We need the
guidance of the
Holy Spirit at all times,
even in the most
mundane experiences
of life. And He is always
present with us to provide
such everyday
direction.

PART 2

Walking with God the Holy Spirit

The first section of this book—Worshipping God the Holy Spirit—centered on the identity and works of the Holy Spirit. As a divine person of the Trinity who engages in divine works, He is worthy of our worship. This second section turns to how we as Christians are to walk with the Holy Spirit, who fills us with the presence of the triune God (chap. 13), gives us life (chap. 14), and guides us to do God's will (chap. 15).

CHAPTER 13

The Holy Spirit Fills Us with the Presence of the Triune God

As originally created, human beings as divine image-bearers were intended to be the people of God. As their Creator, God would dwell with them to glorify Himself and promote their flourishing. Adam and Eve walked with God in the garden of Eden, the place of His dwelling with them. As part of the curse for their disobedience to His moral law, yet also as an act of mercy, God expelled the now-fallen couple [here, the focus is on Adam] from the garden:

> The LORD God sent him away from the garden of Eden to work the ground from which he was taken. He drove the man out and stationed the cherubim and the flaming, whirling sword east of the garden of Eden to guard the way to the tree of life. (Gen. 3:23–24)

Ever since that tragic day, an urgent question has echoed: "Will God yet again dwell with his people?"[1] From beginning to end, Scripture develops a positive answer.

An example of God's dwelling with His people follows the redemption of the Israelites from Egypt. God instructs Moses to build a tabernacle, with this promise:

> "I will dwell among the Israelites and be their God. And they will know that I am the Lord their God, who brought them out of the land of Egypt, so that I might dwell among them. I am the Lord their God." (Exod. 29:43–46)

Another example is God's promise to His people for their obedience to His covenant with them:

> "I will place my residence [that is, dwell] among you, and I will not reject you. I will walk among you and be your God, and you will be my people. I am the LORD your God, who brought you out of the land of Egypt, so that you would no longer be their slaves. I broke the bars of your yoke and enabled you to live in freedom." (Lev. 26:11–13)

In these two examples, God promises to once again dwell with His people.

This dwelling place of God among His people took various forms prior to the coming of Jesus Christ: the tabernacle, Solomon's

---

1. Some of this material is adapted from Gregg R. Allison, *The Church: An Introduction* (Wheaton, IL: Crossway, 2021), 36–41.

temple, and the post-exilic temple.[2] And the prophets sounded a note of hope: one day, God would save His people Israel, overcome their alienation, and once again dwell among them. For example, Zechariah offered this promise:

> "Daughter Zion, shout for joy and be glad, for I am coming to dwell among you"—this is the LORD's declaration. "Many nations will join themselves to the LORD on that day and become my people. I will dwell among you, and you will know that the LORD of Armies has sent me to you. The LORD will take possession of Judah as his portion in the Holy Land, and he will once again choose Jerusalem. Let all humanity be silent before the LORD, for from his holy dwelling he has roused himself." (Zech. 2:10–13)

The Old Testament offered hope of God once again dwelling with His people.

The beginning of the fulfillment of this hope took place in the incarnation of the Word of God, who is the eternal Son:

> In the beginning was the Word, and the Word was with God, and the Word was God. . . . The Word became flesh and dwelt among us. We observed his glory, the glory as the one and only Son from the Father, full of grace and truth. (John 1:14)

The eternal Son—the Word who existed even before the beginning (= the creation)—became the incarnate Son—the Word who

---

2. Unlike the case with the tabernacle and temple, however, the glory of God was never present in this post-exilic structure.

became flesh. As the God-man, He dwelt among the divine image-bearers whom He had created. The incarnation was a clear answer to the question: "Will God yet again dwell with His people?"

Jesus physically lived among His people. While He did, He continued and heightened God's promise of dwelling with His people. Jesus pledged, "If anyone loves me, he will keep my word, and my Father will love him, and we will come to him and make our home with him" (John 14:23). Jesus promised that He and the Father would dwell with Jesus's followers. But how would such an intimate indwelling be possible?

Prior to His promise, Jesus had explained to His disciples: "I will ask the Father, and he will give you another Helper, to be with you forever, even the Spirit of truth. . . . You know him, for he dwells with you and will be in you" (John 14:16–17 ESV). Though the disciples were not strangers to the Holy Spirit, a day was coming in which the Spirit would indwell them. Thus, the dwelling of the Father and the Son in believers would be connected to the indwelling of the Holy Spirit. This fulfilled promise means that the Holy Spirit renders the presence of the triune God.

"Will God yet again dwell with His people?" Yes, through His indwelling Holy Spirit!

The intimacy of God's dwelling with His people is underscored by Jesus in His High Priestly prayer for the unity of His followers:

> "May they all be one, as you, Father, are in me and
> I am in you. May they also be in us, so that the
> world may believe you sent me. I have given them
> the glory you have given me, so that they may be
> one as we are one. I am in them and you are in me,
> so that they may be made completely one, that the

world may know you have sent me and have loved
them as you have loved me." (John 17:21–23)

Jesus prays for unity, that His disciples may "all be one"—
"completely one." Remarkably, this oneness mirrors the oneness
that exists between the Father and the Son; Jesus's disciples are to
be one as the Father and the Son are one. The Father is "in" the Son
as the Son is "in" the Father. Similarly, Jesus's disciples are to be "in"
the Father and the Son. Again, Jesus highlights how this indwelling is possible: Jesus is "in" His disciples and, because the Father
is "in" Jesus, both the Father and the Son are "in" the disciples.
Bringing in our discussion immediately above, this intimate one-
ness/dwelling of the Father and the Son with Jesus's followers is due
to the indwelling presence of the Holy Spirit in Christians. And the
outcome of this unity between Christians is that nonbelievers take
notice and believe that the Father sent the Son and loves them as
the Father loves the Son.

Paul's prayer echoes Jesus's prayer: "I pray that he [the Father]
may grant you, according to the riches of his glory, to be strength-
ened with power in your inner being through his Spirit, and that
Christ may dwell in your hearts through faith" (Eph. 3:16–17). The
association is notable: the Father, the Son, the Holy Spirit, and the
"inner being" of Christians. The triune God dwells with His people. Again, the Holy Spirit is key as Paul addresses the Christians at
Corinth, "Don't you know that your body is a temple of the Holy
Spirit who is in you, whom you have from God?" (1 Cor. 6:19).
Each Christian is a temple of the Holy Spirit.

This indwelling is not just true individually. As we saw in chapter 11, it's also true corporately, that is, true of the church. In his
instructions to the leaders of the Corinthian church, Paul explains
that the church itself is the temple of the Holy Spirit: "Don't you

yourselves know that you [the church] are God's temple and that the Spirit of God lives in you? If anyone destroys God's temple, God will destroy him; for God's temple is holy, and that is what you are" (1 Cor. 3:16–17). The church is the temple of the Holy Spirit.

Important for our purposes, as Paul sees it, the church is the contemporary fulfillment of the promises made long ago:

> What agreement does the temple of God have with idols? For we are the temple of the living God, as God said:
>
> > "I will dwell
> > and walk among them,
> > and I will be their God,
> > and they will be my people.
> > Therefore, come out from among them
> > and be separate, says the Lord;
> > do not touch any unclean thing,
> > and I will welcome you.
> > And I will be a Father to you,
> > and you will be sons and daughters to me,
> > says the Lord Almighty."
>
> So then, dear friends, since we have these promises . . . (2 Cor. 6:16–7:1)

"Will God yet again dwell with His people?" Yes! As God Himself promised. And it is true both individually, for each and every Christian, and corporately, for the church of Christ. Christians and their church are temples of the Holy Spirit.

This calls for reflection for both yourself and your church.

1. What are the key differences between God's presence in the tabernacle and temple and His presence in you individually and in your church?

2. How is your oneness with the Father and the Son through the Holy Spirit similar to the unity between those three persons of the Trinity? How is it different? Why is it important to know both the similarities and the differences?

3. When non-Christians look at your church, do they see an intimate unity that prompts them to wonder about Jesus? What can your church do to enhance its unity?

4. How does/should the work of the Holy Spirit to render the presence of the triune God affect how you and your church are to be and live?

CHAPTER 14

The Holy Spirit Gives Life as We Walk with Him

In light of the work of the Holy Spirit to render the presence of the triune God for believers and their church, how are we to be and live? Scripture's answer is that we are to be filled with the Spirit, walk by the Spirit, keep in step with the Spirit, and set one's mind on the Spirit.[1] Scripture uses these various images to paint a picture of what it looks like to live in the Holy Spirit.

> We are to be filled with the Spirit, walk by the Spirit, keep in step with the Spirit, and set one's mind on the Spirit.

---

1. For further discussion, see Gregg R. Allison and Andreas J. Köstenberger, *The Holy Spirit: Theology for the People of God* (Nashville: B&H Academic, 2020), 403–6.

Be Filled with the Spirit

First, we are to be filled with the Spirit, as we are commanded:

> Don't get drunk with wine, which leads to reckless living, but be filled by [with] the Spirit: speaking to one another in psalms, hymns, and spiritual songs, singing and making music with your heart to the Lord, giving thanks always for everything to God the Father in the name of our Lord Jesus Christ, submitting to one another in the fear of Christ. (Eph. 5:18–21)

There are four key points to our understanding of this passage.

First, "be filled with the Spirit" is a command. It's not a suggestion, nor a promise, nor a warning. Rather, it's an imperative that calls for one of two responses: Obedience, of course, is the intended and proper response (and it will bring good consequences). Disobedience, though a choice that Christians can make, is not the intended and proper response (and it will have bad consequences).

Second, "be filled with the Spirit" is a particular kind of command. It's ongoing, operative throughout each moment of our life. It's not a "do this once and never do it again" type of imperative (like "apply for a social security number"). Rather, it is continuous command and could be paraphrased "keep on being filled with the Spirit" as a way of life.

Third, "be filled with the Spirit" is a command that demands a certain posture: yieldedness to the Spirit. It's not an active voice imperative like "toss me the ball" or "get the book off the shelf and bring it to me." Both these commands require some concrete action in terms of obedience. But Paul's command is a passive voice imperative like "sense the music" or "brace yourself." Both these commands require adopting a certain posture rather than a concrete action.

So it is with "be filled with the Spirit." Obedience to this command demands a posture of yieldedness, submission, and openness to the leading of the Spirit. For me, it's obeyed as I stumble out of bed in the morning and cry, "Spirit, fill me!" That cry says nothing at all about the day that is about to unfold before me. It says nothing whatsoever about the relationships, tasks, ministries, joys, and heartaches that await me throughout the day. More important, it places me in a position of submission to the Spirit and what He will direct me to do throughout the day.

Some Christians insist that "be filled with the Spirit" is a command to read the Bible and pray. Certainly, it is well and good to engage in those activities! But those actions are not the proper response to Paul's command, which requires putting ourselves in a position of yieldedness to the Spirit. So be filled with the Spirit AND read the Bible AND pray!

Still other Christians urge caution with addressing the Holy Spirit directly with the cry, "Spirit, fill me!" Believing that all prayer should be directed to God the Father, they encourage this prayer of obedience to Paul's command: "Father, graciously send Your Holy Spirit to be present with me and to empower me throughout my upcoming day." That is most certainly a fine prayer! In whatever form our obedience may take, our posture of submission to the leading of the Spirit should be true of us each and every moment of our day.

Fourth, "be filled with the Spirit" is a command that, when obeyed, produces certain results and demands certain actions. Immediately following his command, Paul lists four activities (which can be summed up in a word or two):

- speaking to one another in psalms, hymns, and spiritual songs (deep fellowship)
- singing and making music with your heart to the Lord (authentic worship)
- giving thanks always for everything (gratitude)
- submitting to one another in the fear of Christ (honor)

Taking each point in order, when Christians are filled with the Spirit—when together their church is filled with the Spirit—they will enjoy deep, abiding, genuine fellowship. Their community will not be a façade or settle for superficiality. Additionally, they will experience authentic, heartfelt worship of the Lord. Their devotion to Him will not merely go through the motions or settle for entertainment. Moreover, they will live joyfully with constant gratitude, giving thanks both in the good times as well as the bad times. Finally, they will honor one another, showing respect for one another, deferring to one other, preferring others above themselves, and yielding to one another as is fitting for Christians.

This good fruit of genuine fellowship, sincere worship, gratitude, and mutual honor grows when Christians are filled with the Spirit as a church. Rather than merely settling back and experiencing these good results, however, Christians receive this instruction as action points to bring about through the Spirit's empowerment. That is, Christians filled with the Spirit work hard together as a church to build solid community, worship with genuine devotion, overcome grumbling and replace it with thanksgiving, and humbly honor others above themselves. Thus, while filled with the Spirit, together as the church they expect this good fruit to grow. And they use their gifts and abilities so that this good fruit grows (Eph. 4:15–16).

We are to "be filled with the Spirit."

Walk by the Spirit and Keep in Step with the Spirit

Second and third, we are to "walk by the Spirit" and "keep in step with the Spirit," as we are commanded:

> I say, then, walk by the Spirit and you will certainly not carry out the desire of the flesh. For the flesh desires what is against the Spirit, and the Spirit desires what is against the flesh; these are opposed to each other, so that you don't do what you want. But if you are led by the Spirit, you are not under the law.
>
> Now the works of the flesh are obvious: sexual immorality, moral impurity, promiscuity, idolatry, sorcery, hatreds, strife, jealousy, outbursts of anger, selfish ambitions, dissensions, factions, envy, drunkenness, carousing, and anything similar. I am warning you about these things—as I warned you before—that those who practice such things will not inherit the kingdom of God.
>
> But the fruit of the Spirit is love, joy, peace, patience, kindness, goodness, faithfulness, gentleness, and self-control. The law is not against such things. Now those who belong to Christ Jesus have crucified the flesh with its passions and desires. If we live by the Spirit, let us also keep in step with the Spirit. Let us not become conceited, provoking one another, envying one another. (Gal. 5:16–26)

The contrast between life in the Spirit and life in the flesh, or sinful nature, couldn't be more stark—and the consequences of each more serious for eternal life or eternal death!

While the command "be filled with the Spirit" emphasizes the indwelling presence of the Holy Spirit, Paul's second and third imperatives focus on the pilgrimage on which Christians journey throughout their lifetime. As they walk in this world, Christians are to be accompanied by the Spirit and not lag behind or run ahead of the Spirit.

As before, the nature of Paul's instruction is an ongoing command. It is to be obeyed moment by moment. The choice with which Christians are faced consists of two different pathways that are absolute polar opposites to each other. As Paul explains it, Christians can either "walk by the Spirit" or give into and thus "carry out the desire of the flesh," that is, their sinful nature. The intended and proper response is that they walk by the Spirit and thus resist the lure of their sinful nature. This right choice will bring good consequences. The alternative, though a choice Christians can make, is not the intended and proper response. It's that they walk according to the desire of their sinful nature. This wrong choice will bring bad consequences.

Obedience to the command means that Christians will please the Lord and, in so doing, actually do the good things that they really want to do. This lifestyle, which both pleases God and pleases them, is due to the fact that "those who belong to Christ Jesus have crucified the flesh with its passions and desires." With a new nature that has been freed from sin and its carnal urgings—remember our discussion about regeneration—they want more than anything else to please God and do good. And so they live, walking by the Spirit. In terms of concrete results, they manifest the fruit of the Holy Spirit—Christlike character and virtues. Though not mentioned, the eternal outcome is eternal life in God's kingdom.

Disobedience to the command means that they will displease the Lord and, in so doing, actually do the bad things they really don't want to do. Again, this confusion is due to the fact that (apparently) they are born again and have a new nature that wants to avoid sinning. In terms of concrete results, those who walk according to their sinful nature will manifest the works of that nature—ungodly character and vices. Tragically, it may turn out that, in reality, these people were never genuine disciples of Jesus Christ. For them, the warning is startling: the eternal outcome is exclusion from the kingdom of God.

The choice is clear: walk by the Spirit and live, or walk according to the sinful nature and die.

As he concludes his directive to walk by the Spirit and thus live, Paul alters the image a bit: "If we live by the Spirit, let us also keep in step with the Spirit. Let us not become conceited, provoking one another, envying one another." This third imperative—"keep in step with the Spirit"—is a command for Christians to travel in lockstep with the Spirit. They are not to lag behind the Spirit's leading, nor are they to run ahead of His guidance. They are to keep up with Him, following Him wherever He takes them.

> The choice is clear: walk by the Spirit and live, or walk according to the sinful nature and die.

Paul mentions three areas that are opposites of keeping in step with the Spirit. Pride—thinking more highly of oneself than one ought to think—is ruled out. Provocation—disturbing or unsettling others—is wrong. Envy—desiring what others are or have—is precluded. These relationship breakers are clearly "works of the flesh." Those who exhibit pride, provocation, and envy do not "keep in step with the Spirit." We are to "walk by the Spirit" and "keep in step with the Spirit."

Set One's Mind on the Spirit

Fourth, and in a way highly reminiscent of his imperative to "walk by the Spirit," Paul commands Christians to "set your mind on the Spirit." This command has specific reference to doing the moral will of God so as to please Him.

> For what the law could not do since it was weakened by the flesh, God did. He condemned sin in the flesh by sending his own Son in the likeness of sinful flesh as a sin offering, in order that the law's requirement would be fulfilled in us who do not walk according to the flesh but according to the Spirit. For those who live according to the flesh have their minds set on the things of the flesh, but those who live according to the Spirit have their minds set on the things of the Spirit. Now the mindset of the flesh is death, but the mindset of the Spirit is life and peace. The mindset of the flesh is hostile to God because it does not submit to God's law. Indeed, it is unable to do so. Those who are in the flesh cannot please God. (Rom. 8:3–8)

Once again, the contrast between setting one's mind on the things of the flesh (sinful nature), or setting one's mind on the things of the Spirit, is a night-and-day difference.

First, Paul rehearses what God has done in Christ to accomplish salvation for sinful people. Through the atoning sacrifice of Christ,

God has freed Christ's followers to fulfill the righteous requirement of God's moral law. That is, Christians may do God's will—love God, love others, refuse to return evil for evil, turn the other cheek, bear with one another, and much more—and thus please Him.

Second, Paul underscores *how* Christians may fulfill God's moral law. It is certainly not by walking according to their flesh—erecting idols to replace God, disrespecting others, living sensually, stirring up divisions, and much more. It is certainly not by setting their mind on the things of their sinful nature. On the contrary, Christians fulfill their duty by walking according to the Spirit. They are able to please God by setting their minds on (the things of) the Spirit. Though it probably goes without saying, "setting one's mind on the Spirit" is not just about thinking rightly. It involves a whole-person submission to Him.

Paul underscores the choice Christians have moment by moment. It is centered on what their mind centers on: either on the sinful nature or on the Spirit. The intended and proper response is that Christians set their mind on the Spirit. Connecting with earlier commands, the obedient choice is "be filled with the Spirit," "walk by the Spirit," and "keep in step with the Spirit." The alternative, though a choice Christians can make, is not the intended and proper response. It's that they set their mind on their sinful nature. Again, connecting with earlier commands, the disobedient choice is neglecting the filling of the Spirit and walking according to the desires of the flesh.

The choice is a matter of life and death. Setting one's mind on the things of the flesh results in death because such a centering leads to hostility toward God and rebellion against His moral law. Indeed, the flesh-centered person cannot submit to the law and, as a result, cannot please God. Oppositely, setting one's mind on the things of the Spirit results in life and peace. Gone is hostility, rebellion, and disobedience. In their place is the freedom to fulfill the righteous requirement of the moral will of God. We are to set our mind on the Spirit.

Heeding these similar directives—be filled with the Spirit, walk by the Spirit, keep in step with the Spirit, and set one's mind on the Spirit—calls for application.

1. What does being filled with the Holy Spirit look like concretely in your life?

2. How can you more consistently walk by the Spirit so as not to give into the desires of your sinful nature?

3. What are the biggest obstacles to your keeping in step with the Holy Spirit? What concrete plan can you develop to overcome these obstacles so as to live more consistently in the Holy Spirit? (Remember: *doing more* is not necessarily a good plan.)

4. How can you ensure that "setting your mind on the Spirit" does not just become an intellectual exercise—a matter of right thinking only—but engages the entirety of your life and effort?

CHAPTER 15

The Holy Spirit Guides
Us to Do God's Will

At the start of chapter 2, I asked a question: As you look back over the course of your Christian life, how can you account for the growth that you see? Of course, it was a leading question, intended to focus your attention on the presence and power of the Holy Spirit.

Let me alter the question a bit: As you look back over the course of your Christian life, how can you account for the places, schooling, training, responsibilities, ministries, and people that are so crucial to your story? (Like before, it is a leading question.) Can you at least answer in part that the direction that your life has taken is due to the presence and guidance of the Holy Spirit? That is, the development of your life and the elements in it—your friendships, spouse (if you are married), job, church involvement, joys, heart-aches, and more—can be traced to the leading of the Spirit.

I begin with a personal story. When we were engaged and only a few weeks before being married, Nora and I were visiting a businessman and his wife in a small town near South Bend, Indiana. We had received permission from Campus Crusade for Christ (now Cru) to begin support raising for our upcoming ministry. As we shared our future work with this couple, the man jokingly said, "Wouldn't it be interesting if you were assigned to the University of Notre Dame?" As Notre Dame is in South Bend, Indiana, his question made initial sense. But on further reflection, we wondered what would Cru, a Protestant evangelistic ministry, be doing on the premier Roman Catholic university in America? We enjoyed a good laugh, finished sharing about our work (wherever it would be), and said our goodbyes.

As I climbed into the driver's seat of our 1966 Oldsmobile and Nora got into the passenger seat, we turned to each other and said, "God is calling us to the University of Notre Dame." It was not an audible voice that we heard, nor was there some kind of writing on the dashboard that we read. Rather, it was a firm conviction that we would end up with Cru at Notre Dame.

After the flurry of activity of a wedding and honeymoon, we arrived at Cru's headquarters in San Bernardino, California. Part of our initial staff training included filling out a ministry placement form. That is, we were asked where in the world we would like to end up on staff. Of course, we wrote down "the University of Notre Dame."

A few days passed before we were called into the placement office. As Cru leaders explained, they were intrigued by our interest in going to Notre Dame because the Cru ministry was just beginning there. They were actually looking for other staff to join the small pioneering team.

They also informed us that we would not be a part of that team. They gave us three reasons. First, we didn't have a Roman Catholic background, which they as Cru leaders considered to be crucial for an assignment at ND. Second, as newly married, we didn't have any children. Because the small team in place at Notre Dame was a couple with two children, the Cru leaders wanted us to have a similar lifestyle as those we would be joining. Third, Cru only launches new campus ministries with veteran staff people—and we were rookies. They informed us that we would not be assigned to ND.

About ten days later, we were given another ministry placement form to complete. Again, we wrote down "the University of Notre Dame." That same day we were called down to the placement office. "What didn't you understand by the word 'not' when we told you that you would *not* be assigned to Notre Dame?" our supervisors asked kindly.

Another ten days passed and there was a third placement form to fill out. Our answer was more complete this time around: "We will go anywhere that Cru assigns us, but we truly believe that God is calling us to the University of Notre Dame." Only a few hours passed this time before we had our final conversation with Cru leaders. "Maybe God is calling you to Villanova University," they offered, "or to some other Catholic institution, but you are not going to be assigned to the University of Notre Dame!"

A few days passed and on the final night of our training, we were handed our ministry assignment letter in a sealed envelope. The instructions were to find an isolated location, open the envelope, find out our staff assignment, and observe a twenty-four-hour period of silence to pray about the assignment before talking to anyone else about it. As we sat under the palm trees and tore open the envelope, we read our assignment: the University of Notre

Dame! As soon as the time period expired, we met with Cru leaders. They told us that our clear call to go to ND outweighed all their objections to assigning us to that ministry.

How can we explain that clarity of direction in any way other than attributing it to the presence and guidance of the Holy Spirit?[1]

You may be thinking, *So what's the big deal? That has happened to me on more than one occasion, so I agree with you.* Others may be feeling, *I'm not so sure that God directs in such a dramatic way these days. I've never experienced such a thing, so I have some doubts and suspicions.* Still others may be sure that what we experienced was due either to peer pressure or to indigestion from the pepperoni pizza we ate. You would explain, *While the Holy Spirit did indeed directly guide people in the early church (as we read in the New Testament), He doesn't direct people in such a way in our post-New Testament times.*

So the guidance of the Holy Spirit as it pertains to life and ministry is a controversial topic. Let's think about it carefully.

As always, let's begin with Scripture. We do indeed find the Holy Spirit directly guiding people in the early church. As one example, we take the narrative of Paul, Timothy, and Silas as they embarked on the second missionary journey:

> [Paul, Timothy, and Silas] went through the region of Phrygia and Galatia; they had been forbidden by the Holy Spirit to speak the word in Asia. When they came to Mysia, they tried to go into Bithynia, but the Spirit of Jesus did not allow them. Passing by Mysia they went down to Troas.

---

1. For further discussion, see Gregg R. Allison and Andreas J. Köstenberger, *The Holy Spirit: Theology for the People of God* (Nashville: B&H Academic, 2020), 400–403.

> During the night Paul had a vision in which a Macedonian man was standing and pleading with him, "Cross over to Macedonia and help us!" After he had seen the vision, we immediately made efforts to set out for Macedonia, concluding that God had called us to preach the gospel to them. (Acts 16:6–10)

This report of the initial travels of Paul, Timothy, and Silas is shocking!

As a bit of context, this group had been called by the Holy Spirit and commissioned by the church of Antioch to embark on a missionary journey to preach the gospel and plant churches. The three set out to travel west through Asia but ended up taking a detour north into Phrygia and Galatia. The reason: the Holy Spirit forbade them to carry out their ministry in Asia. This Spirit-prevention is shocking because He had called them to preach the gospel and plant churches. Amazingly, however, He was telling them, "No, not here, not now!"

As they continued traveling north through Mysia toward Bithynia, they took a detour west. The reason: the Holy Spirit did not allow them to carry out their ministry in that direction. Again, this Spirit-blockade is shocking because He had called them to preach the gospel and plant churches. Amazingly, however, He was telling them the same thing: "No, not here, not now!"

Journeying west, the group came to Troas, a port city. God gave Paul a night vision of a man of Macedonia (a region to the northwest and across the sea from Troas) calling for help. Obediently, the group "sought to go on into Macedonia, concluding that God had called us to preach the gospel to them." Setting out by boat, they made an island stop on Samothrace, then sailed to Neapolis. Back on foot, they traveled to Philippi, a leading city of Macedonia.

The stage was set with everything in place:

> On the Sabbath day we went outside the city gate by the river, where we expected to find a place of prayer. We sat down and spoke to the women gathered there. A God-fearing woman named Lydia, a dealer in purple cloth from the city of Thyatira, was listening. The Lord opened her heart to respond to what Paul was saying. (Acts 16:13–14)

Paul and his missionary band had been called by the Spirit and sent by the church of Antioch to preach the gospel and plant churches. In obedience to this commission, they had journeyed a very long way—400 miles!—on foot and by boat not preaching the gospel and not planting churches. Shocking, indeed! But why? Because the Holy Spirit prevented them from engaging in their missionary task, saying, "No, not here, not now." Only when they arrived at the Spirit's intended audience and destination—Lydia and Philippi— did the Spirit grant them permission—"Yes, here and now"—to preach the gospel and start a church: the church of Philippi.[2]

As you read my retelling of this narrative, you will probably find yourself aligning with one of five distinct positions regarding the guidance of the Holy Spirit for life and ministry.

  • This guidance was reserved for the apostles alone. Being limited to the apostles (the

---

2. Another narrative of the guidance of the Holy Spirit for ministry is the account of the conversion of the Ethiopian eunuch (Acts 8:26–40).

Twelve, minus Judas, plus Matthias and Paul),
it doesn't continue today.

- This guidance was reserved for the apostolic
age (the first century) alone. It was mostly
for the apostles but some (many?) others as
well (for example, Barnabas, James, Timothy,
Titus). Being limited to the first century, it
doesn't continue today.

- This guidance was particularly for the apostolic age (the first century), but may continue
in a modified form today. That is, such guidance may be expressed less frequently today
than it was in the first century, less strongly
today than it was then, and/or is more for
church leaders than church members today.

- This guidance is for the age of the Spirit (the
time between the first and second coming of
Christ). Therefore, it continues today, yet in
a modified form. That is, such guidance is
expressed less frequently today than it was in
the first century, less strongly today than it
was then, and/or is more for church leaders
than church members today.

- This guidance is for the age of the Spirit (the
time between the first and second coming of
Christ). Therefore, it continues today as it did
in the apostolic age.

Though we will return to this question below, what is your
view of the guidance of the Holy Spirit for life and ministry?

As you ponder the Spirit's guidance, a few points are important to keep in mind. First, Scripture itself recounts some dramatic experiences of the Spirit's leading. For example, when the Holy Spirit rushed upon him, Samson engaged in savage actions: he tore apart a roaring lion (Judg. 14:5–6) and killed thirty men of Ashkelon (vv. 10–20). Even more, though tied up, Samson snapped the ropes binding him and slayed 1,000 Philistines with the fresh jawbone of a donkey—because "the Spirit of the LORD came powerfully on him" (15:9–17).

As another example, the sons of the prophets tried to figure out Elijah's disappearance; he had been taken up "into heaven by a whirlwind" (2 Kings 2:11). They offered a guess: "Maybe the Spirit of the LORD has carried him away and put him on one of the mountains or into one of the valleys" (2 Kings 2:16). Though their idea was wrong, it does imply that the Spirit could act dramatically.

A final example is Philip. Not only did the angel of the Lord and the Holy Spirit dramatically direct Philip in his encounter with the Ethiopian eunuch. As Philip baptized the new believer, "when they came up out of the water, the Spirit of the Lord carried Philip away, and the eunuch saw him no more. . . . But Philip found himself at Azotus" (Acts 8:39–40). "Carried away" seems to have been a remarkable snatching up of Philip and relocating him.

Dramatic experiences of the Spirit's guidance are not unheard of in Scripture. At the same time, we should not become enamored with spectacular events such as these examples. We need the guidance of the Holy Spirit at all times, even in the most mundane experiences of life. And He is always present with us to provide such everyday direction.

As a second point to consider, Scripture doesn't glaze over the difficulty in discerning the guidance of the Holy Spirit. In Acts

19–21, Luke recounts four related stories of the Spirit's leading. In the first, Paul resolves in the Spirit to go to Rome via Jerusalem (19:21). In the second story, Paul senses that the Holy Spirit is constraining him to travel to Jerusalem, where imprisonment and affliction awaited (20:22–4). In the third, when Paul visits the believers in Tyre, they plead with him "through the Spirit" not to go to Jerusalem (21:4–5). In the fourth story, Agabus prophesies by the Holy Spirit. He warns Paul that the Jews in Jerusalem will seize and imprison him if he travels there. The Christians with Paul in Caesarea understand this

> We need the guidance of the Holy Spirit at all times, even in the most mundane experiences of life. And He is always present with us to provide such everyday direction.

warning to be a word from the Spirit. They urge their dear friend—who is himself urged by the Spirit to go to Jerusalem—not to undertake the journey and thus risk his life (vv. 11–12).

Importantly, Luke doesn't resolve the tension that is present in these related stories. Paul senses the leading of the Holy Spirit to go to Jerusalem. Moreover, he knows through the Spirit that trouble awaits him there. The Christians in Tyre, through the Holy Spirit, plead with him not to go. The same is true of the Christians in Caesarea when they hear the prophetic word of the Spirit through Agabus. So who is being guided by the Holy Spirit? It seems all those involved. Ultimately, his friends entrust Paul to the Lord's will, and he travels to Jerusalem and his destiny there.

This unresolved tension should be comforting to Christians today. At times, some may sense the guidance of the Spirit in one direction, while others may understand the Spirit is leading in a different direction. In fact, that has been my experience, and I guess it has been yours as well. So rather than despair and fear, we should continue to seek to discern the voice of the Holy Spirit.

Affirming the Spirit's guidance even in the midst of tension raises a practical question: How are we to discern whether it is the Spirit who is leading or if the direction is merely the result of our imagination—or of something more insidious? I offer seven criteria to help in the process of discerning the leading of the Holy Spirit.

The first is completely subjective: We must be *"in the Spirit"* in order to discern the voice of the Spirit. This point harkens back to the earlier discussion of being filled with/walking by/keeping in step with/setting one's mind on the Holy Spirit. Unless we adopt a posture of yieldedness to the Spirit, we should not expect Him to guide us clearly or grant us discernment regarding His direction.

> We must be *"in the Spirit"* in order to discern the voice of the Spirit.

Criteria two through seven, which I offer in the form of questions, are objective. Still, they require us to be "in the Spirit" as we answer the questions.

Second, *Scripture* is our criterion: Is such perceived guidance by the Spirit of God in accordance with the inspired Word of God? This is not a call for proof texting or wrongly interpreting a biblical passage so as to justify the supposed leading of the Spirit. Though we may not be able to point to a specific passage, can we determine that the true voice of the Spirit is in keeping with a biblical precedent or a biblical pattern?

The third criterion is *Jesus Christ*: Does such alleged direction of the Spirit exalt Jesus Christ? If part of the Spirit's work is to glorify the Son of God, it would stand to reason that any direction that we sense from the Spirit would lead us to honor Him. Such promotion of Christ would stand in contrast with an alleged voice that would foster one's own reputation and/or promote one's own fame.

Fourth, the Spirit's work of *sanctification* is our criterion: Does such perceived guidance of the Spirit stimulate progress in holiness? After all, He is the *Holy* Spirit, so we should expect that His direction will further our progress in walking in the way that Christ walked.

The fifth criterion is *missionality*: Does the guidance that we sense from the Spirit encourage and empower us to engage others with the gospel? Christ promised the Holy Spirit so that the church would receive power to be His witnesses everywhere (Acts 1:8). So it would make sense that His leading would further the church's missional work to make disciples of all the nations.

The sixth criterion focuses on *the church*: Does the church community—especially its leaders and those members who know the person well—confirm this alleged direction of the Spirit? Far too often today, Christians dismiss any external authority and accountability. Perhaps they have been wrongly thwarted from carrying out God's will by a carnal, Spirit-insensitive church. Having encountered such an obstacle, Christians have the tendency to avoid their church's counsel and charge ahead without being assessed and sent out by their community. But the church's confirmation of the leading of the Spirit serves as a protection against misguided enthusiasm or insistence on getting one's way at all costs.

The seventh and final criterion is *the Spirit Himself*: Will the perceived direction of the Spirit likely bear the fruit of the Spirit and His virtues? These include "love, joy, peace, patience, kind-ness, goodness, faithfulness, gentleness, and self-control" (Gal. 5:22–23); "righteousness, peace, and joy" (Rom. 14:17); "hope" (Rom. 15:13); and much more.

Time for some application.

1. What is your view of the guidance of the Holy Spirit for life and ministry? Which of the five positions most closely describes your view? Why?

2. As we noted, the guidance of the Holy Spirit as it pertains to life and ministry is a controversial topic. Why is it important that Christians and their churches don't dismiss or condemn those who hold a different position than they do?

3. Do you find the seven criteria for discerning the guidance of the Spirit helpful? Why or why not? Can you think of other criteria that should be added to this list? Are you in a situation that calls for discernment using these criteria?

4. How is your church doing in sensing the guidance of the Spirit and helping its members discern His leading? Are there ways you can strengthen your church in this area?

The church
should strive to
arrange for spiritually gifted
members to use their particular
gift(s) in ministries that call
for the exercise of
those gifts.

PART 3

Working with God the Holy Spirit

The first section of this book—Worshipping God the Holy Spirit—centered on the identity and works of the Holy Spirit. As a divine person of the Trinity who engages in divine works, He is worthy of our worship. The second section addressed how we as Christians are to walk with the Holy Spirit, who fills us with the presence of the triune God, gives us life, and guides us to do God's will. This third section, which begins with a brief chapter (16) about the Spirit's work before the incarnation of the Son and the outpouring of the Spirit on Pentecost, focuses on how we work with the Holy Spirit by using His gifts (chap. 17), some of which are debated (chap. 18).

CHAPTER 16

The Earlier Work of the Holy Spirit

Before we turn our attention to working with the Holy Spirit today, we need first to know that His present work didn't begin two thousand years ago with the incarnation of the Son and the Spirit's outpouring on the day of Pentecost. Certainly, those events draw our attention to the Spirit's mighty power: He was the one who brought about the Son's incarnation and energized the Son's mission—mission 1. And the Spirit was the one whom the Father and the Son poured out on Pentecost, inaugurating the Spirit's mission—mission 2. But by no means was the Spirit inactive before these earthshaking events! But what was the nature of His earlier work?

First, from the very outset of our world, the Holy Spirit was active in its creation (Gen. 1:1–2):

> In the beginning God created the heavens and
> the earth. Now the earth was formless and empty,
> darkness covered the surface of the watery depths,

and the Spirit of God was hovering over the surface of the waters.

The original state of the earth was without structure, void of life,
dark (so nothing could be seen, like what cave explorers experience when they turn off their lights), and without a solid foundation. In other words, there was no point of reference in this original
creation, which was completely inhospitable to plants, fish, birds,
animals, and—to say the least—people.

Over this rough and not-ready original creation, the Holy Spirit
hovered like a strong bird protecting and preparing its young. He
was readying this unformed and empty earth for God's imminent
work of three days of forming—the first three days—and three
days of filling—the next three days. In the process, light would
dispel the darkness. Solid ground would anchor the water and be
its boundary. The Holy Spirit would prepare the crude, raw materials for God's transformation of them from wild space to hospitable
place. So, when God spoke:

1. "Let there be light"
2. "Let the water under the sky be gathered into
   one place, and let the dry land appear"
3. "Let the earth produce living creatures according to their kinds"

the Holy Spirit prompted the obedient response from the creation
He had prepared, corresponding to the above:

1. "And there was light"
2. "And it was so"
3. "And it was so"

The Holy Spirit was active in the work of original creation.

Second, in relation to the people of Israel, the Holy Spirit would come upon their leaders to empower them to carry out their specific tasks. Those leaders included judges, kings, and prophets.

> 1. Judges
>
> The Holy Spirit would stir up judges, empowering them as military commanders to turn back Israel to the Lord. One example is Othniel:
>
> > The Israelites did what was evil in the Lord's sight; they forgot the Lord their God and worshiped the Baals and the Asherahs. The Lord's anger burned against Israel. . . . The Israelites cried out to the Lord. So the Lord raised up Othniel . . . as a deliverer to save the Israelites. *The Spirit of the Lord came on him, and he judged Israel.*[1] (Judg. 3:7–10)
>
> 2. Kings
>
> The Holy Spirit would come upon Israel's kings, anointing them to lead the people. An example is David:
>
> > The Lord said [to Samuel], "Anoint him [David], for he is the one [to become king]." So Samuel took the

---

1. Other examples of the Holy Spirit empowering judges to defeat Israel's enemies include Ehud (Judg. 3:12–20); Gideon (6:11–7:25); and Jephthah (11:6–9 with 11:29–33).

horn of oil and anointed him in the
presence of his brothers, and *the
Spirit of the LORD came powerfully on
David from that day forward.* (1 Sam.
16:13)

3. Prophets

The Holy Spirit would speak through the
prophets, revealing God's ways, the sinfulness
of the people, the future, and much more. An
example is Ezekiel:

[The Lord] said to me [Ezekiel],
"Son of man, stand up on your feet
and I will speak with you." As he
spoke to me, *the Spirit entered me*
and set me on my feet, and I listened
to the one who was speaking to me.
He said to me, "Son of man, I am
sending you to the Israelites . . . *and
you must say to them, 'This is what
the Lord GOD says.'* Whether they listen or refuse to listen—for they are
a rebellious house—they will know
that a prophet has been among them.
(Ezek. 2:1–5)[2]

---

2. Another example of the Holy Spirit speaking through the prophets is
Micah (Mic. 3:8); more generally, all the prophets "were carried along by the
Holy Spirit" (2 Pet. 1:16–21).

The Holy Spirit would come upon judges, kings, and prophets, empowering these leaders to carry out their tasks of leading Israel to military victory, ruling the people, and speaking God's Word.

Third, this Old Testament emphasis on the work of the Holy Spirit among the leaders of Israel should not lead us to conclude that He was inactive in the lives of the other "common" people. Graciously, the earlier work of the Spirit brought salvation to them. We can't imagine anyone being forgiven of sins, growing in holiness, worshipping God, loving His Word, and trusting God to fulfill His promises apart from the work of the Spirit. So, it was the Spirit's action that rescued and consecrated the people of God.

> It was the Spirit's action that rescued and consecrated the people of God.

An example is Simeon (Luke 2:25–28): "This man was righteous and devout, looking forward to Israel's consolation, and *the Holy Spirit was on him*. It had been *revealed to him by the Holy Spirit* that he would not see death before he saw the Lord's Messiah. *Guided by the Spirit*, he entered the temple." Taking Jesus in his arms, Simeon praised God for fulfilling His promise of the Messiah. So, though the Old Testament focuses on the Spirit's work among judges, kings, and prophets, this emphasis by no means implies that the Spirit was inactive among the "common" people of God to turn them to the Lord and consecrate them as genuine worshippers. The Holy Spirit was active in salvation.

Fourth, and as I introduced in chapter 8, there is an important theme that courses through the Old Testament: the promise of a future, unprecedented work of the Holy Spirit in association with a Spirit-anointed Suffering Servant/Messiah. He would introduce a new covenant that would be characterized by the presence and power of the Spirit.

Jeremiah prophesied that this unparalleled work would be part of a new covenant that God would establish with His people (Jer. 31:31–34). Featured prominently in this new covenant would be the forgiveness of sin. Ezekiel promised that this unprecedented work, in addition to a purification from all sins, would feature an internal renewal—a new heart. Moreover, God would put the Holy Spirit within His people, thereby enabling them to obey His moral law and please Him (Ezek. 36:25–27). Joel heightened this theme through his prophecy that God would pour out His Spirit "on all humanity"—men and women, young and old, slave and free (Joel 2:28–29). One day, then, the people of God would be filled with the presence and power of the Holy Spirit.

For this vision to become a reality, God would provide a Spirit-anointed Messiah. As Isaiah describes the future Messiah, he links Him closely with the Holy Spirit:

> Then a shoot will grow from the stump of Jesse,
> and a branch from his roots will bear fruit.
> *The Spirit of the* Lord *will rest on him—*
> a Spirit of wisdom and understanding,
> a Spirit of counsel and strength,
> a Spirit of knowledge and of the fear of the
>   Lord. . . .
> He will judge the poor righteously
> and execute justice for the oppressed of the land.
>   (Isa. 11:1–2, 4)

Isaiah repeats this link between the Suffering Servant and the Holy Spirit. As the Lord declares:

"This is my servant; I strengthen him,
this is my chosen one; I delight in him.
I have put my Spirit on him;
he will bring justice to the nations." (Isa. 42:1)

As the Messiah Himself underscores, He will execute justice through the Spirit who anoints Him:

The Spirit of the Lord GOD *is on me,*
because the LORD has anointed me
to bring good news to the poor.
He has sent me to heal the brokenhearted,
to proclaim liberty to the captives
and freedom to the prisoners;
to proclaim the year of the LORD's favor.
(Isa. 61:1–2)

It is this passage to which Jesus turns when He preaches in the synagogue at the beginning of His ministry (Luke 4:16–21). As the fulfillment of these promises, Jesus is the Spirit-anointed Messiah who would bring salvation to the people of God.

The work of the Holy Spirit would be decisive for the mission of the Messiah.

But how did the eternal Son of God become incarnate as the God-man Jesus so as to accomplish this saving work?

> The Holy Spirit worked powerfully to bring about the incarnation.

Fifth, for these prophecies to be fulfilled, the Holy Spirit worked powerfully to bring about the incarnation. As Matthew narrates,

> The birth of Jesus Christ came about this way: After his mother Mary had been engaged to Joseph, it was discovered before they came together that *she was pregnant from the Holy Spirit.* So her husband, Joseph, being a righteous man, and not wanting to disgrace her publicly, decided to divorce her secretly.
>
> But after he had considered these things, an angel of the Lord appeared to him in a dream, saying, "Joseph, son of David, don't be afraid to take Mary as your wife, because *what has been conceived in her is from the Holy Spirit.* She will give birth to a son, and you are to name him Jesus, because he will save his people from their sins." (Matt. 1:18–21)

Twice in this short story Matthew emphasizes that the incarnation of the Son did not come about by normal sexual intercourse between Mary and Joseph. Rather, the incarnation was wrought by the Holy Spirit.

Luke's Gospel underscores the same powerful work of the Holy Spirit. Following the angel's announcement that she would become the mother of the Lord,

> Mary asked the angel, "How can this be, since I have not had sexual relations with a man?" The angel replied to her, "*The Holy Spirit will come upon you, and the power of the Most High will overshadow you.* Therefore, the holy one to be born will be called the Son of God." (Luke 1:34–35)

Though a virgin, and thus not capable of becoming pregnant, Mary would accomplish her God-given role of becoming the mother of the incarnate Son through the powerful work of the Holy Spirit.

The Holy Spirit's work effected the incarnation of the Son of God.

Sixth, the Holy Spirit did not only inaugurate the eternal Son's existence as the incarnate Son. The Spirit also filled the God-man with His presence and power throughout Jesus's earthly life and ministry. Jesus's anointing with the Spirit was exactly in accordance with the Old Testament's prophecies about the Suffering Servant/Messiah.

Specifically, God the Father poured out the Holy Spirit on His Son "without measure" (John 3:34). This Spirit-anointing began from the moment of the Son's incarnation and was vividly manifested when Jesus was baptized by John the Baptist:

> When all the people were baptized, Jesus also was baptized. As he was praying, heaven opened, and the Holy Spirit descended on him in a physical appearance like a dove. And a voice came from heaven: "You are my beloved Son; with you I am well-pleased." (Luke 3:21–22)

As John, the one who baptized Jesus, testified (John 1:32), "I saw the Spirit descending from heaven like a dove, and he rested on him." The fact that the Spirit descended and rested on Jesus means that Jesus was enriched with the constant and all-sufficient empowering presence of the Spirit. Certainly, the Son and the Spirit are eternally related as persons of the Trinity. The incarnation and descent of the Spirit on Jesus did not at all change that eternal relation. Still, at Jesus's baptism, the Spirit was poured out and rested on the incarnate Son in an unprecedented way. The God-man was now empowered for His role as the Spirit-anointed Messiah to do His work of salvation.

Relying on the Holy Spirit throughout His earthly life and ministry, Jesus faced down temptations from Satan (Mark 1:12–13) and all the trials and tests that came His way. In the power of the Holy Spirit, Jesus proclaimed the gospel (Luke 4:18–19, citing Isa. 61:1–2), teaching in parables, calling the crowds to follow Him, instructing His disciples, challenging the errant traditions of the religious leaders, and predicting His own death and resurrection. Filled with the Holy Spirit without measure, Jesus exorcised demons (Matt. 12:22–31), releasing the victims of the evil one from its fierce and destructive domination (Mark 5:1–20). Energized by the Holy Spirit, Jesus performed miracles (Acts 10:37–38), restoring sight to the blind (John 9:1–7), causing the lame to walk (Mark 2:1–12), cleansing the lepers (Luke 5:12–16), healing the sick (Matt. 4:23), feeding the five thousand (John 6:5–14), raising the dead (Mark 5:21–43), and much more.

> God the Father poured out the Holy Spirit on His Son "without measure" (John 3:34).

As throughout His life, so as His days on earth were coming to an end, Jesus was guided by the Spirit to "set his face to go to Jerusalem" (Luke 9:51 ESV). There, Jesus would face His death by crucifixion, be buried, and rise again, in accordance with His own predictions (Matt. 16:21; 17:22–23; 20:17–19). As He walked on the torturous path to fully accomplish His mission, Jesus relied step-by-step on the Spirit who constantly and sufficiently filled Him.

Through the Spirit, Jesus handed the morsel of bread to Judas (John 13:26–27); submitted to Judas the betrayer's kiss (Luke 22:48–50); reprimanded Peter for his futile combative tactic (John 18:10–11); looked at Peter who had denied him (Luke 22:54–62); responded forthrightly to Annas the high priest (John 18:19–24); engaged Pilate in a conversation about kingship and truth (18:33–38); remained silent before Herod (Luke 23:8–9); carried his cross part way to Golgotha (John 19:17); comforted the weeping daughters of Jerusalem (Luke 23:27–31); and promised paradise to the repentant thief (Luke 23:39–43).[3]

Even Jesus's death by crucifixion was accomplished through the Holy Spirit: "Christ . . . through the eternal Spirit offered himself without blemish to God" (Heb. 9:14). "As in life, so in death, God the Son incarnate, anointed with the Spirit without measure, depended on the Spirit to carry out his mission of salvation."[4]

Having sacrificed Himself to pay the penalty for the sins of fallen people, Jesus rose from the dead. His resurrection was also the work of the Holy Spirit and

> As He walked on the torturous path to fully accomplish His mission, Jesus relied step-by-step on the Spirit who constantly and sufficiently filled Him.

---

3. Adapted from Gregg R. Allison and Andreas J. Köstenberger, *The Holy Spirit: Theology for the People of God* (Nashville: B&H Academic, 2020), 358–59.

4. Allison and Köstenberger, *The Holy Spirit*, 359.

foreshadowed the resurrection of all who trust in Jesus and His salvation (Rom. 8:11): "If the Spirit of him [God the Father] who raised Jesus from the dead lives in you, then he [God the Father] who raised Christ from the dead will also bring your mortal bodies to life through his Spirit who lives in you." As God the Father raised Jesus Christ from the dead by the power of the Holy Spirit, so, too, will God raise Jesus's followers from the dead through the indwelling Spirit.

With the resurrection goes the ascension; the Spirit-anointed incarnate Son completed His mission by returning to heavenly glory as the God-man. Now He reigns as the cosmic head over all creation and as the head of the church in particular (Eph. 1:20–23).

The Holy Spirit's presence in and powerful work through the incarnate Son was the foundation for the entire earthly life and ministry of Jesus Christ, including His death, resurrection, and ascension.

Seventh, we know these wonderful truths about the earlier work of the Holy Spirit through the Bible. "All Scripture is inspired [or breathed out] by God" (2 Tim. 3:16). This work of inspiration has special reference to the Spirit: the biblical authors "spoke from God as they were carried along by the Holy Spirit" (2 Pet 1:21). Though this passage has particular reference to the writing of the Old Testament, the Spirit's work of inspiration continued in the writing of the New Testament. It is to this New Testament that we turn to understand the Holy Spirit's present work in the giving of gifts to Christians and the church.

Time for some questions for application.

1. Why is it important to remind yourself that the work of the Holy Spirit did not begin two thousand years ago with the

incarnation of the Son and the Spirit's outpouring on the day of Pentecost?

2. How does Jesus's constant and complete dependence on the presence and power of the Holy Spirit throughout His earthly life and ministry serve as a model for your dependence on the Spirit moment by moment?

3. It is sometimes thought that in the times of Jesus's deepest need—His temptation in the wilderness, for example, or His painful toil in hanging on the cross—the Holy Spirit abandoned Him so that Jesus had to face those temptations and troubles as merely a man. Such withdrawal of the Spirit served to prove that Jesus was fully human. Thus, He can serve as the perfect model of obedience and faith for us who do not have special divine help to rescue us out of our difficulties. How does this chapter expose the error of this kind of thinking?

CHAPTER 17

The Present Work of the Holy Spirit in Giving Gifts

As noted in chapter 11, the Spirit plays a vital role in the building up of the church. Church members, endowed with spiritual gifts and empowered by the Spirit, use them to deepen and expand the ministries of the church.[1]

In terms of a basic definition, spiritual gifts are the Holy Spirit's endowments of believers. For a fuller definition, I turn to Sam Storm's idea in *Understanding Spiritual Gifts*: "spiritual gifts are capacities or abilities imparted to Christians by the Holy Spirit to enable them to exceed the limitations of their finite humanity in

---

1. For further discussion see Gregg R. Allison and Andreas J. Köstenberger, *The Holy Spirit: Theology for the People of God* (Nashville: B&H Academic, 2020), 426–34; Gregg R. Allison, *Sojourners and Strangers: The Doctrine of the Church*, Foundations of Evangelical Theology (Wheaton, IL: Crossway, 2012), 413–24; Gregg R. Allison, *The Church: An Introduction* (Wheaton, IL: Crossway, 2021), 127–30, 146–52.

order to serve other believers to the glory of God."[2] These gifts are from the Holy Spirit; thus, they are "spiritual" gifts. They are capabilities distributed to all church members; every Christian has at least one gift. While they may be similar to natural abilities—think of skill in teaching and in administrating—spiritual gifts function in ways beyond natural capacities. When Christians use their gifts, the result or fruit exceeds what would normally occur if they were simply natural talents operating on a human plane of effectiveness. In this sense, then, all spiritual gifts are supernatural. Indeed, Christians are to use their spiritual gifts for a dual outcome: to serve other Christians by helping the church to mature and multiply, and to bring honor to the Lord.

Scripture addresses spiritual gifts in four principal passages: Romans 12:4–8; 1 Corinthians 12–14; Ephesians 4:7–16; and 1 Peter 4:10–11. It presents various purposes for them. The first and foremost purpose is to build up the church so that it matures and multiplies. Paraphrasing Paul's words, "to each [church member] is given the manifestation of the Spirit [that is, the member's spiritual gift] for the common good [of the whole church]" (1 Cor. 12:7). While church members may derive personal benefit when they use their gift or gifts, that is a bonus outcome. Spiritual gifts are not intended for personal growth or self-aggrandizement. Rather, their purpose is to benefit the church so that it becomes more like Jesus Christ and expands throughout the world.

---

2. Sam Storms, *Understanding Spiritual Gifts: A Comprehensive Guide* (Grand Rapids: Zondervan, 2020), 18. He calls this definition the common or traditional view. He includes a modified definition later in his discussion: "A spiritual gift is when the Holy Spirit manifests his presence and imparts his power into and through individual believers to enable them to exceed the limitations of their finite humanity so that they might faithfully and effectively fulfill certain ministry tasks for the building up of the body of Christ" (20).

Scripture presents other purposes for spiritual gifts. A second use was the confirmation of the gospel message and its messengers (Heb. 2:1–4). As the apostles and their associates preached the good news about Christ, how were their original hearers to know that their message was truly from God? How were their audiences to know that Peter, John, Paul, and the others were the God-appointed messengers to bring the gospel? As they proclaimed salvation in Jesus, "God also testified by signs and wonders, various miracles, and distributions of gifts from the Holy Spirit according to his will" (v. 4). Spiritual gifts confirmed the message and messengers of the gospel.

A third purpose is to give the church a glimpse of the much-expanded work of the Holy Spirit that is to come when Christ returns. We rightly marvel when we see the Spirit at work as Christians exercise their gifts. At the same time, we are reminded that the joyous fruit that we see now pales in comparison with the fulness of the presence and power of the Holy Spirit in the age to come.

Finally, a fourth use is to manifest the ascended Christ's victory over His enemies. As Paul explains about Jesus, "When he ascended on high, he led a host of captives, and he gave gifts to men" (Eph. 4:8 ESV, alluding to Ps. 68:18). Not only did the once-crucified and resurrected Jesus ascend to take His proper place at the right hand of God the Father. The ascension also marked Christ's victory over all His enemies and, in His exaltation, He gave gifts to His church: apostles, prophets, evangelists, pastors, and teachers (Eph. 4:11). Interestingly, then, the Bible indicates that both Christ and the Holy Spirit distribute spiritual gifts (though it tends to emphasize this giving as the work of the Spirit).

Having defined what they are and noted their purposes, what are the gifts that the Spirit gives? I present a modified list of spiritual gifts from Sam Storms's, *Understanding Spiritual Gifts*, adding my definitions to the gifts:

- *prophecy:* reception of a revelation from God that is then communicated to the church, which, in turn, evaluates it
- *service:* any general act of ministry, perhaps overlapping with the gift of helping (see below)
- *teaching:* communication of biblical truth and sound doctrine, together with the ability to refute false teachers and heresies
- *exhortation:* encouragement of members to become fully devoted followers of Christ and admonition to the church toward maturity and multiplication
- *contributing/giving:* whereas all Christians are commanded to give sacrificially for the furtherance of the ministry and care of the poor, these givers contribute a substantially higher percentage of their wealth and possessions
- *leading:* setting and advancing the direction of the church
- *mercy:* acts of compassion for the relief of church members and of the poor and marginalized
- *word of knowledge:* communication of messages that go beyond the ordinary means of human intelligence and learning

- *word of wisdom:* communication of messages that go beyond the ordinary means of human prudence and judgment
- *faith:* advancement of the will of God by an overcoming and persistent trust in Him to fulfill His promises for the church and its purposes
- *gifts of healing(s):* acts of physical restoration that overcome sickness and injury
- *miracles:* acts of power (like resurrection and deliverance from persecution) for the advancement of God's kingdom
- *distinguishing of spirits:* discerning whether it is the Holy Spirit or a demonic spirit(s) that is exerting influence over a person or a situation
- *tongues:* communication of encoded speech—perhaps a language with which one is unfamiliar, or an encrypted utterance—that rehearses God's mighty acts, expresses mysteries toward God, and/or voices prayers that bypass one's mind
- *interpretation of tongues:* explanation or translation of what is spoken in tongues (see previous), thereby rendering that speech intelligible to the church
- *helping:* supporting those in need, perhaps through financial relief or physical assistance
- *administrating:* designing, developing, and executing church ministries while managing members involved in them

- *evangelizing:* engaging in sharing the gospel
  with those outside the church on a frequent
  basis and perhaps being unusually fruitful in
  leading others to Christ
- *shepherding:* discipling others through one-
  on-one mentoring, small group discipleship,
  and/or leading a church through pastoring its
  members

Perhaps you're wondering why a few familiar "gifts" are not in this list. I turn to a discussion of the gifts of apostle/apostleship, pastoring or pastors and teachers, hospitality, craftsmanship or artistry, and marriage and singleness/celibacy.

Though *apostle/apostleship* could be a spiritual gift (1 Cor. 12:28), it is closely tied to the office of apostle.[3] Additionally, it is part of the list of "gifted people" whom Jesus gave to His church (Eph. 4:11). Thus, apostle/apostleship seems more an office or position than a spiritual gift.[4] Similarly, *pastoring* (1 Pet. 5:1–2) or *pastors and teachers* (Eph. 4:11) are often listed as a spiritual gift. For the same reason as just noted, it may be better to see this as a reference to an office. Using *shepherding* in place of *pastoring* also allows us to distinguish between qualified men who hold the office

---

3. The apostles were those called by Jesus (Mark 3:13–15), described as "the Twelve" (Matt. 26:20), yet included others beyond that initial group, like Paul and Barnabas (Acts 14:14).

4. I appreciate much of the current discussions about "apostolic gifting" and "apostolic ministry" that detach *apostle* from the office held by Peter, John, Paul, and the others and use it to describe leaders of church-planting movements and networks. A pioneer in this development is Alan Hirsch, *The Forgotten Ways: Reactivating the Missional Church* (Grand Rapids: Brazos Press, 2006). For a different perspective, see Matt Rhodes, *No Shortcut to Success: A Manifesto for Modern Missions* (Wheaton, IL: Crossway, 2022).

of pastor and both women and men who have the gift of shepherding (that is, disciple-making) but are not pastors in the sense of
office holders.

More likely to be a spiritual gift is *hospitality*. Though all
Christians are called to be hospitable—that is, to open their hearts
and their homes to strangers—some Christians excel in this virtue.
As Peter commands in a long list of exhortations:

> Be hospitable to one another without complain-
> ing. Just as each one has received a gift, use it to
> serve others, as good stewards of the varied grace
> of God. If anyone speaks, let it be as one who
> speaks God's words; if anyone serves, let it be from
> the strength God provides. (1 Pet. 4:9–11)

The closeness of Peter's treatment about hospitality to his instruction about using one's spiritual gift is an indicator that hospitality is
indeed a gift from the Holy Spirit.

Also likely to be a spiritual gift is *craftmanship* or *artistry*. For the
construction of the tabernacle, the Holy Spirit filled Bezalel with
"wisdom, understanding, and ability in every craft to design artistic
works in gold, silver, and bronze, to cut gemstones for mounting,
and to carve wood for work in every craft" (Exod. 31:3–5). The
Spirit also filled Oholiab and his pupils "with skill to do all the
work of a gem cutter; a designer; an embroiderer in blue, purple,
and scarlet yarn and fine linen; and a weaver. They can do every
kind of craft and design artistic designs" (Exod. 35:34–35). Today,
these skills may be spiritual gifts that advance the church's building
and maintenance as well as enhance its worship service through
visual and performing arts.

Both *marriage* and *singleness/celibacy* are "gifts" (1 Cor. 7:7). But this idea of gifting is clearly different from spiritual gifts in the sense we are discussing them. It doesn't belong in this category.

The Holy Spirit has given followers of Jesus Christ one or more gifts! How, then, do we identify which gift or gifts we have?

- prophecy
- service
- teaching
- exhortation
- contributing/giving
- leading
- mercy
- word of knowledge
- word of wisdom
- faith
- gifts of healing(s)
- miracles
- distinguishing of spirits
- tongues
- interpretation of tongues
- helping
- administrating
- evangelizing
- shepherding

Other possible gifts:

- apostleship/apostle
- pastoring or pastors and teachers
- hospitality
- craftsmanship/artistry

One way of discovery is to do a spiritual gift inventory. This survey—and there are varieties of them—aims to help church members identify their gift(s). It asks for responses—for example, "never true of me," "sometimes true of me," "always true of me"—to multiple statements—for example, "I regularly share the gospel with unbelievers" and "I weep over and pray for those who don't yet know Christ." The responses are tallied, and the inventory suggests what gift or gifts that member has. For example, if there is a regular pattern of "always true of me" to statements about evangelism and the unreached, the inventory would indicate that evangelism is likely the member's spiritual gift. Like any tool, this assessment instrument can be used well or poorly.

Another way of identifying one's gift(s) is for members to take on the responsibility of helping each other to know their gift(s) as they work together in ministry. For example, after a member of a Sunday school class does a particularly adept job of communicating the truth of a biblical passage, members of the class comment, "Thanks for helping me know God better through your lesson. Could it be that you have the gift of teaching?" Similarly, after a member leads a meeting particularly well, the participants comment, "Did you see how you guided us from chaos to consensus? Do you think you have the gift of leading?" Mutual encouragement can go far in helping church members identify their gift(s). When that support from others is accompanied by a sense of satisfaction on the part of the one who teaches/leads, members gain a strong assurance of their gifting.

Rather than musing about our gift(s), we should engage in ministry wherever it's needed. Again, Sam Storms urges:

> Open your eyes and look for those who are weeping. Ask the Spirit to guide your steps to those

> who are weak, afflicted, and destitute. . . . Look
> for those in financial straits and give to them gen-
> erously. Identify the despairing and speak words
> of encouragement. When people are drifting,
> open your Bible and teach them truth. . . . Instead
> of first asking, "What is my gift?", ask the ques-
> tion, "Who is in need?" . . . If we would devote
> ourselves to praying, giving, helping, teaching,
> serving, and exhorting those around us, the like-
> lihood greatly increases that we will walk head-
> long into our gifting without ever knowing what
> happened.[5]

As we actively work in various ministries, our gift(s) will become evident.

Once members have identified their gift(s), their church has the responsibility to train them how to use them. Some people might object: "If they are gifts of the Spirit, why would they need development?" Importantly, spiritual gifts come with both a divine dimension and a human dimension. As for the former, the Spirit distributes the gifts and empowers them. There's nothing that the church can add to His divine work. As for the latter, the human dimension means that church members with the gift of teaching teach, and those with the gift of leading lead, and those with the gift of exhortation exhort, and the like. Teachers can be trained to teach better. Leaders can be trained to lead better. Exhorters can be trained to exhort better. This human dimension is the responsibility of the church.

---

5. Sam Storms, "10 Questions about Spiritual Gifts" (September 5, 2020), https://www.crossway.org/articles/10-questions-about-spiritual-gifts/.

Having identified their gift(s) and been trained to use them, church members should engage in ministries in which they will best and most regularly use their gift(s). Again, this utilization of members according to their gifting is the church's responsibility. Certainly, it is the case that the nursery needs people to wipe runny noses and hold crying infants. That need must be filled, whether by members who have the gift of helping or who have the gift of teaching. Church ministries need able-bodied people, whatever their gift(s) may be. Still, the church should strive to arrange for spiritually gifted members to use their particular gift(s) in ministries that call for the exercise of those particular gifts. That should be the goal.

Time for application.

1. What is your gift or gifts? How do you know? How does your gift(s) become manifested in ministry in your church? Are there some ministries in which you should be active so that you can use your gift(s) more?

2. What can you do to develop your gift(s)?

3. Does your church promote spiritual gifts? That is, does your church help its members identify their gift(s), then train its members to use their gift(s), and finally deploy its members in ministries that need them to use their gift(s)? Are there ways in which you can help your church develop in this area?

CHAPTER 18

The Holy Spirit and His Debated Gifts

Everything discussed in the previous chapter is rather noncontroversial. Certainly, there is debate about the definition of some of the gifts and whether or not spiritual gift inventories are good or bad. But these are not major disagreements. This chapter tackles a much deeper and long-lasting debate over certain gifts of the Spirit.

This debate is between two positions: cessationism and continuationism.[1] It plays off the distinction between so-called "sign" or "miraculous" gifts and the other gifts. In the first category are seven gifts:

---

1. Some of this material is adapted from Gregg R. Allison, *The Church: An Introduction* (Wheaton, IL: Crossway, 2021), 146–52. See also Gregg R. Allison, *Sojourners and Strangers: The Doctrine of the Church*, Foundations of Evangelical Theology (Wheaton, IL: Crossway, 2012), 413–24.

Category 1

prophecy

word of knowledge

word of wisdom

healings

miracles

speaking in tongues

interpretation of tongues

In the second category are twelve gifts:

Category 2

service

teaching

exhortation

contributing/giving

leading

mercy

faith

distinguishing of spirits

helping

administrating

evangelism

shepherding

Continuationism holds that all the nineteen gifts—those from both categories—continue today. *Cessationism* believes that the seven gifts in the first category have ceased today. Only the twelve gifts in the second category operate today.

We begin with the area of agreement. All churches, whether they hold to continuationism or cessationism, concur that the Holy Spirit distributes the twelve spiritual gifts—those in the second category—to church members today.

Next is the area of disagreement. Here is the center of debate. Churches that hold to continuationism maintain that the Holy Spirit *continues* to distribute all the nineteen spiritual gifts—those from both categories—to church members today. Churches that hold to cessationism maintain that the Holy Spirit has *ceased* to distribute the seven spiritual gifts—those from the first category—to church members today.

Both positions deserve an extended treatment.

Continuationism holds that all the nineteen spiritual gifts continue today. Importantly, there is a spectrum of continuationist views:

- *minimum* continuationism: affirms belief in the operation of all the gifts but never practices gifts like prophecy and healing in the church. This view is functional cessationism.
- *medium* continuationism: affirms belief in the operation of all the gifts and occasionally practices gifts like prophecy and healing

in the church. Some call this view "open but cautious."[2]

- *maximum* continuationism: affirms belief in the operation of all the gifts and regularly practices gifts like prophecy and healing in the church. This position is functional continuationism.

- *manic* continuationism: affirms belief in the operation of all the gifts and irresponsibly (that is, with little regard for biblical guidelines) practices gifts like prophecy and healing in the church. An example would be the "word of faith" movement.

We'll return to this question later, but if you hold to continuationism, where do you place yourself on this spectrum?

Proponents offer six arguments in favor of continuationism:

First, though it is not their only purpose, the primary purpose of spiritual gifts is to build up the church so that it matures and multiplies. We can assess this reality in two ways. No matter the condition of an individual church or of the church in general, each church and the church as a whole falls woefully short of the biblical vision. Thus, all the gifts are needed today and continue to be distributed by the Holy Spirit.

Second, and in accord with this first reason, Scripture implies that all the spiritual gifts continue until Christ's return ("the revelation/the day of our Lord Jesus Christ" [1 Cor. 1:7–8]). Additionally,

2. Robert L. Saucy, "An Open but Cautious View," in *Are Miraculous Gifts for Today?: Four Views*, gen. ed. Wayne A. Grudem (Grand Rapids: Zondervan, 1996), 95–172.

Scripture indicates that certain spiritual gifts (prophecy, knowledge, speaking in tongues) will cease at that event (1 Cor. 13:8–12), not before. If these gifts are representative of the seven "debated" gifts in the first category, then the Spirit continues to give all the spiritual gifts to the church. Moreover, He will continue to do so until Christ comes again.

Third, historical evidence for the continuation, rather than the cessation, of such gifts as prophecy, healings, and miracles is strong from the end of the first century to today.[3] Thus, one of the reasons offered in support of cessationism—that the seven category 1 gifts were confined to the apostles and the age in which they lived (the first century)—fails. Historical evidence contradicts this alleged support and backs continuationism.

Fourth, the category 1 gifts, while prominent among the apostles, were never confined to them. Certainly, "the signs of an apostle . . . signs and wonders and miracles" (2 Cor. 12:12) operated in Peter, John, Paul, and the other apostles. But those gifts were not limited to them. Stephen, a deacon, performed "great wonders and signs" (Acts 6:8). So, too, did Philip, also a deacon (Acts 8:6–7). Philip's four virgin daughters prophesied (Acts 21:8–9), as did unnamed women members of the church of Corinth (1 Cor. 11:5–6) who also spoke (as did some men) in tongues (1 Cor. 14). God gave the Galatian church the Holy Spirit and worked miracles among its members (Gal. 3:5). Prophecy, tongues, miracles—these signs were not confined to the apostles but seem to have been commonplace in the church.

---

3. For further discussion, see Stanley M. Burgess and Eduard M. van der Maas, eds., *The New International Dictionary of Pentecostal and Charismatic Movements*, rev. ed. (Grand Rapids: Zondervan, 2002), 730–69.

Fifth, and consequently, evidence that these "debated" gifts were limited (even primarily) to the apostles is wrong. The conclusion, then, that cessationism draws—when the apostles died, the gifts associated with them ceased—is incorrect. Thus, an important support for cessationism should be dismissed.

Sixth, continuationism asks a question: What would have signaled to the church—say, at the end of first century, or the middle of the fourth century—that it was no longer obligated to obey the following New Testament commands about prophecy and speaking in tongues?[4]

- "Pursue love and desire spiritual gifts, and especially that you may prophesy" (1 Cor. 14:1).
- "Be eager to prophesy, and do not forbid speaking in tongues" (1 Cor. 14:39).
- "According to the grace given to us, we have different gifts: If prophecy, use it according to the proportion of one's faith" (Rom. 12:6).
- "Don't stifle the Spirit. Don't despise prophecies, but test all things. Hold on to what is good" (1 Thess. 5:19–21).

These commands are similar to the more common commands like: "warn those who are idle, comfort the discouraged, help the weak, be patient with everyone" (1 Thess. 5:14) and "pray without ceasing" (1 Thess. 5:17 ESV).[5] At the same time, they are quite dif-

---

4. For further discussion, see Andrew Wilson, *Spirit and Sacrament: An Introduction to Eucharismatic Worship* (Grand Rapids: Zondervan, 2019), 108.

5. These commands are immediately before the commands listed above in 1 Thessalonians 5:19–21.

ferent from clearly limited commands like: "When you come, bring the cloak I left in Troas with Carpus, as well as the scrolls, especially the parchments" (2 Tim. 4:13). So, after the death of the apostles, how would the church have known not to give heed to these apostolic commands about spiritual gifts? If the reply is "nothing would have so signaled," then the ongoing nature of those commands supports continuationism.

To sum up, continuationism has strong support.

Cessationism holds that the seven gifts in the first category have ceased. Only the twelve gifts in the second category operate today. Importantly, there is a spectrum of cessationist views:

- *interruptive* cessationism: while affirming generally that cessationism is the case, this view allows for the possibility that the Holy Spirit occasionally distributes one or more of the seven gifts, as the need arises and for a limited period of time.

- *regionalized* cessationism: while affirming generally that cessationism is the case, this view allows for the possibility that the Holy Spirit distributes one or more of the seven gifts in certain areas of the world. These regions are those in which pioneering missionary work goes on and Scripture is not yet widely available to the new churches being established.[6]

---

6. This category has some resemblance to Tom Schreiner's "nuanced cessationism" view. Thomas R. Schreiner, *Spiritual Gifts: What They Are and Why They Matter* (Nashville: B&H Publishing Group, 2018), 165.

- *absolute* cessationism: affirms that cessationism is the case, and anyone who claims to
  have any of the seven gifts is either deceived,
  under demonic influence, or is giving in to
  peer pressure to act like they have those gifts.

We'll return to this question later, but if you hold to cessationism, where do you place yourself on this spectrum?

Importantly, and to avoid misunderstanding, "cessationism does not deny that God continues to heal, perform miracles,
and providentially direct His people today. On the contrary, He
may sovereignly intervene in astounding ways whenever and with
whomever He so wills. However, cessationism denies that God
operates in such ways through believers with the gifts of healings,
miracles, and prophecy."[7]

Proponents offer six arguments in favor of cessationism:

First, though not their only purpose, the primary purpose of
spiritual gifts was the authentication of the gospel and its heralds at
the beginning of the church (Heb. 2:1–4). The church's foundation
has been established and the truthfulness of the gospel has been
proven. So, category 1 gifts, having served their purpose, aren't
needed for its maturity and multiplication.

Second, and tied to the first argument, Scripture indicates that
these gifts have ceased. One key passage is Paul's affirmation that
the church is "built on the foundation of the apostles and prophets" (Eph. 2:20). As Tom Schreiner explains with regard to prophets and prophecies, "if such authoritative apostles don't exist today
(and many continuationists agree on this point), and if prophets
spoke infallible words like the apostles, and if the church is built on

---

7. Allison, *The Church: An Introduction*, 149.

the foundation of the apostles and prophets, then there are good grounds to conclude that the gift of prophecy has ceased as well."[8] That is, these gifts of apostleship and prophecy are linked to God's work of revelation. However, such revelatory action stopped when the New Testament was completed (see the discussion below). Some cessationists who appeal to this passage demonstrate that the other gifts like speaking in tongues, interpretation of tongues, healings, and so forth are linked to divine revelation as well. Thus, they conclude that each of the seven gifts, being a gift of revelation, has ceased because God's activity of revelation has concluded. Other cessationists don't make this link and consider the role of gifts like tongues, healings, and miracles to be less important.[9]

Third, another key passage that was used historically in support of cessationism (less so today), indicates that certain spiritual gifts (prophecy, knowledge, speaking in tongues [1 Cor. 13:8]) will cease "when the perfect comes" (1 Cor. 13:10). The "perfect" refers to the close of the canon of Scripture—when God ceased giving revelation in terms of the written Word of God.[10] For some who hold this view, this event occurred at the end of the first century (about AD 96), when the apostle John wrote Revelation, the last of the New Testament writings. For other proponents, this event occurred around the middle of the fourth century (AD 367) when the church acknowledged both the Old Testament and the New Testament as we have them today.[11] That is, the church recognized the Bible was complete. In either case, cessationism emphasizes that

8. Schreiner, *Spiritual Gifts*, 160.

9. For example, Schreiner, *Spiritual Gifts*, 162–64.

10. The canon of Scripture is simply a list of which writings belong in the Bible.

11. Athanasius's *Thirty-ninth Easter Letter* spelled out the canon of Scripture.

prophecy, tongues, and the other gifts linked to revelation have ceased.

Fourth, contemporary cessationism (along with continuation-ism) dissents from that earlier understanding of 1 Corinthians 13 as referring to the close of the canon of Scripture. Paul's phrase "when the perfect comes" (1 Cor. 13:10) refers, instead, to Christ's return. Thus, this passage does not indicate when gifts like tongues, proph-ecy, and so forth will cease. The decision about when they ceased has to be based on other considerations.[12]

Fifth, one such consideration is Paul's note that "the signs of an apostle were performed with unfailing endurance among you, including signs and wonders and miracles" (2 Cor. 12:12). Cessationists hold that the reception and exercise of gifts like prophecy, tongues, and miracles was limited to the apostles. Some would expand this group slightly to include others like Stephen and Philip, associates of the apostles. Thus, once the last of the apostles died, the Holy Spirit ceased distributing these gifts to the church.

As noted in continuationism's fourth argument, continuation-ism disagrees with this evidence. Philip's four daughters prophesied (Acts 21:8–9). The Corinthian church regularly engaged in proph-ecy and speaking in tongues (1 Cor. 11:5–6; chap. 14). The church in Galatia experienced miracles (Gal. 3:5). Prophecy, tongues, mir-acles—these signs were not confined to the apostles but seem to have been commonplace in the church.

Sixth, there is little historical evidence for the continuation of such gifts as prophecy, healings, and miracles from the end of the first century to today. This weak evidence underscores that the

---

12. For further discussion, see Richard B. Gaffin, Jr., "A Cessationist View," in *Are Miraculous Gifts for Today: Four Views*, gen. ed. Wayne A. Grudem (Grand Rapids: Zondervan, 1996), 23–94.

seven "debated" gifts were confined to the apostles and the age in which they lived (the first century). As noted above, continuationism disputes this point.

To sum up, cessationism has strong support.

No matter what our view is, both continuationism and cessationism need to avoid two extremist errors. The first is an underemphasis on spiritual gifts. Along with other good emphases—sound doctrine, gospel-centered preaching, Christ-focused worship services, discipleship, biblical leadership—our churches should teach about spiritual gifts. They should train their members how to use their gifts and deploy members with their gifts in church ministries. Our churches will mature and multiply as their members exercise their spiritual gifts empowered by the Holy Spirit.

Our churches will mature and multiply as their members exercise their spiritual gifts empowered by the Holy Spirit.

A second extremist error is an overemphasis on spiritual gifts. To the neglect of other good emphases—doctrine, preaching, worship, and more—churches emphasize prophecies, speaking in tongues, praying for healing, claiming miracles, and more. In some (many?) cases, these activities violate biblical instructions.[13] Our churches will suffer from chaotic, disordered practices such as these expressions.

These "debated" gifts invite some reflection.

---

13. Examples of biblical instruction (1 Cor. 14:26–35) include two or, at the most, three speaking in tongues (which must be interpreted) and two or, at the most, three communicating their prophecy (which must be evaluated).

1. Do you hold to continuationism or cessationism? What version of this view do you hold? Why?

2. Does your church hold the same position? If it holds the other view, does that create tension for you as a church member? If so, how do you live with that tension?

3. Does your church commit one of the two extremist errors on this topic, either underemphasize or overemphasize spiritual gifts? If so, what can you do to move your church away from its error?

4. Do you think it's possible for these opposing positions to arrive at some kind of consensus? Why would such an agreement—even a partial one—be important for the church of Jesus Christ today?

Conclusion

Thank you for following along as I've shared with you my personal story of discovering the Spirit-filled life. The Holy Spirit is God, gift, and guide!

We are to worship the Holy Spirit, who is the third person of the Trinity, fully God, equal in nature to the Father and the Son. Still, He is distinct from them, being characterized by eternal procession from the Father and the Son. In concert with those two, He engages in mighty acts. His works include speaking, convicting, saving, illuminating, interceding, working in the church, and perfecting all the acts of the triune God. Together with the Father and the Son, He is to be worshipped for who He is and for what He does.

We are to walk with the Holy Spirit moment by moment. He fills us with the presence of the triune God, the fulfillment of promises given long ago. He gives us life as we are filled with the Spirit, walk by the Spirit, and keep in step with the Spirit. He guides us to do God's will. Our posture of yielding to the Spirit prepares and empowers us to resist the lure of our flesh, or sinful nature, and thus to please God fully.

We are to work with the Holy Spirit by using His gifts. These include (among many others) serving, teaching, leading, showing mercy and, from a continuationist perspective (and these gifts are debated), prophecy, speaking in tongues, and healing.

I began this book with a claim: *The greatest gift that God the Father gives to those who follow His Son is the Holy Spirit.* I pray and hope that you agree. More important, I pray and hope you have made the wonderful discovery of the Spirit-filled life. Most important, I pray and hope you will love and adore the Holy Spirit for His presence and not just for His speaking, salvation, power, and gifts.

To God—Father, Son, and Holy Spirit—be the glory in Christ Jesus and in the church!